I0048406

2ND EDITION

Incorporating
Offshore

by Jay Butler
AssetProtectionServices.com

ISBN 978-0-9914644-5-6

INCORPORATING OFFSHORE
COMPLETE GUIDE TO 6 KEY JURISDICTIONS

Table of **Contents**

Disclaimer

Asset Protection Services of America

The inverted "V" displayed on our shield is the uppercase letter "L" in ancient Greek identifying the people of Lacedaemonia, which in historical times was the proper name for the Spartan state. The Greek cry "Molôn Labé" means "Come and Get Them" as spoken by King Leonidas in response to the Persian army's demand for the outnumbered Spartans (300 against 300,000) to surrender their weapons during battle in the narrow pass or 'hot gates' of Thermopylae in 480 B.C. The iconic expression has become a symbol of courage to defend that which belongs to you, even if faced against overwhelming or insurmountable odds.

Author

Jay Butler is the Managing Director of Asset Protection Services of America, the former Managing Director of Asset Protection Services International, Ltd and the former Vice-President of Sales and Marketing for Corporate Support Services of Nevada Inc. Mr. Butler holds a Bachelor's Degree of Fine Arts from Boston University.

Jay has provided customized business entity structuring for clients in all 50 states along with some of the most respected names in the industry including the Jay Mitton organization "the father of asset protection" and Real Estate Investor Association seminars.

While working with Wealth Protection Concepts, LLC under the tutelage of the former Las Vegas and North Las Vegas city attorney Carl E. Lovell Jr. (now deceased from Leukemia), Mr. Butler was bestowed the title of "Asset Protection Planner" for his competency and experience. He also co-authored the first edition of his book "Cover Your Assets: Legal Authorities on Asset Protection, Tax Strategies and Estate Planning" © 2006 with Dr. Lovell.

While residing in Switzerland, Mr. Butler was the Associate Director of "CO-Handelszentrum GmbH" providing Swiss company formation and administration services and executed a full-range of fiduciary responsibilities including sales, client support and international corporate compliance services (KYC, FATCA, AML, FATF and Swiss Code of Obligations).

Jay builds his relationships through consistent attention to detail and reliable support. He has traveled extensively throughout the United States (having visited 49 of the 50 states), explored 36 nations worldwide, and has lived in a total of 7 countries throughout North America, Central America, the Middle East, North Africa and Europe.

Dr Robert Hagopian is semi-retired and the former CEO of Nevada Trustee Services Group Inc, which has provided trustee services to attorneys and law firms throughout the United States since 2005, and the former CEO of the Commerce Bank Ltd in Hong Kong.

Since 1968, Robert has traveled extensively throughout Asia and lived in Japan, Hong Kong and the Philippines with current residency and offices in Manilla.

Dr. Hagopian holds a Bachelor of Science (BS) degree in business administration, an MsD (doctorate) in philosophy and a "jure Dignitatis" Bachelor of Laws degree.

Since 1984, Dr. Hagopian has been structuring business entities for optimum wealth preservation, profitability, asset protection and limiting personal liability through the use of domestic corporations, limited liability companies and various trust vehicles.

Robert has developed innovative processes for the acquisition, holding and marketing of real property. In 2008, Dr. Hagopian applied for the patent-pending "Equity Recovery Program". Based on IRC 351 rules for the transference of real estate to a corporation, the program lawfully avoids capital gains tax, self-employment and state taxes upon the sale of real property.

Contact Us

Please browse our website at www.AssetProtectionServices.com and contact us to schedule your free private asset protection consultation. We welcome the opportunity to hold a 3-way conference call with your tax advisor and/or legal counsel to address any specific questions or concerns you may have. Experience has demonstrated it favorable to have all related parties "on the same page" when creating your structure.

Asset Protection Services of America
701 South Carson Street (Suite #200)
Carson City, Nevada 89701-5239
Office   (775) 461-5255
Skype   Jay_Butler
E-Mail   info@AssetProtectionServices.com
Website www.AssetProtectionServices.com

Books by Jay Butler
and Dr. Robert Hagopian

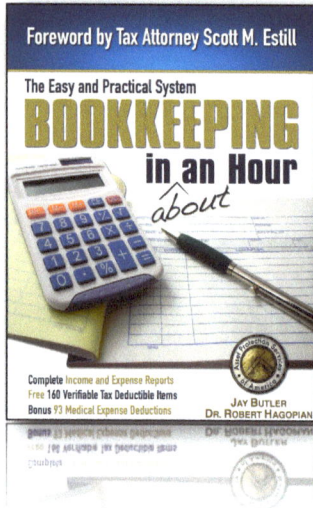

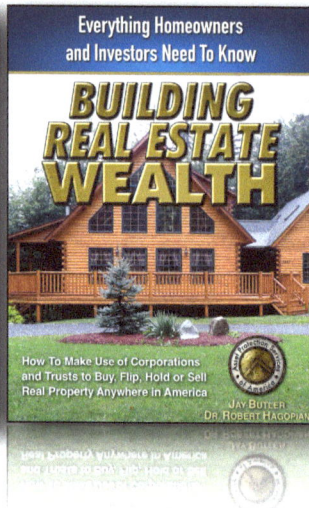

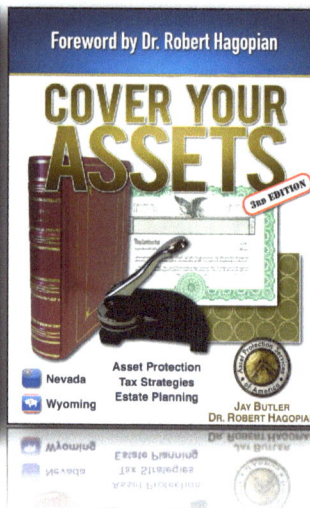

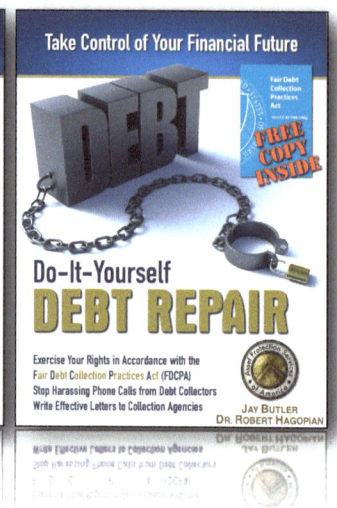

Book	ISBN
Bookkeeping in About an Hour	ISBN 978-0-9914644-0-1
Building Real Estate Wealth	ISBN 978-0-9914644-1-8
Cover Your Assets *(3rd Edition)*	ISBN 978-0-9914644-2-5
Do-It-Yourself Debt Repair	ISBN 978-0-9914644-7-0

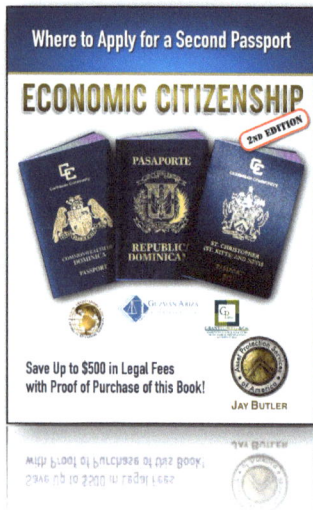

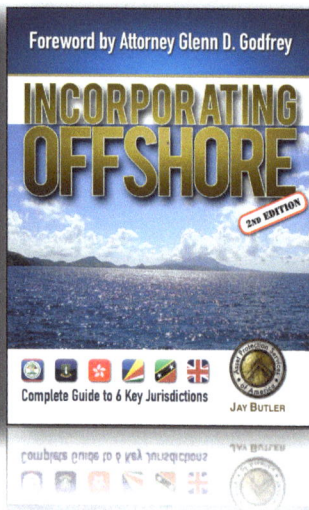

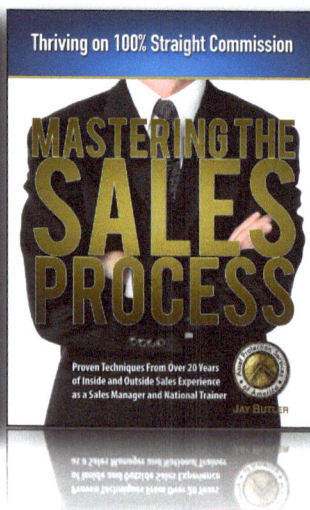

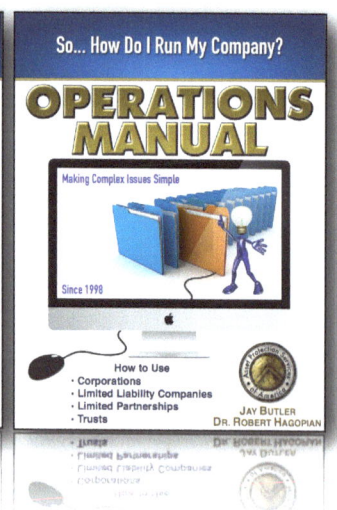

Book	ISBN
Economic Citizenship *(2nd Edition)*	ISBN 978-0-9914644-4-9
Incorporating Offshore *(2nd Edition)*	ISBN 978-0-9914644-5-6
Mastering the Sales Process	ISBN 978-0-9914644-6-3
Operations Manual	ISBN 978-0-9914644-3-2

Foreword

GDG
Glenn D. Godfrey & Company. LLP

Attorneys-at-Law
Patent & Trademark Agents
Notaries Public

Glenn D. Godfrey, S.C.
Estevan A. Perera, B.A., LL.B. (Hons) C.L.E.
Andrew Bennett, LL.B. (Hons), C.L.E.

Jonathan K. Brathwaite BSc LL.B (Hons)
U.K. Representative Office

#35 Barrack Road
P.O. Box 1074
Belize City, Belize

Tel: (Bz City) 501-223-3530/3505
(San Pedro) 501-226-4320
(USA) 832-295-0637
Fax: 501-223-3501
E-mail: attorneys@godfreylaw.net

11th September 2013

Mr. Jay Butler
Via Soldini 14
Chiasso, Ticino
6830 Switzerland (CH)

Dear Mr. Bulter

I have read your pending publication, Incorporating Offshore, in particular your treatment of the Belize International Business Companies Act and the Qualified Retired Persons Act. As a former Attorney General of Belize, I am pleased to endorse and recommend your work. It is a very concise, informative and accurate description of the jurisdiction and the relevant legislation.

The publication will be a valuable addition to the libraries of both service providers and their clients.

We wish you the very best in your effort now and in the future.

Regards,
GLENN D. GODFREY & CO LLP

per: Glenn D. Godfrey S.C.

STATE CAPITAL GROUP   STEP   INTA   International Business Law Consortium

Member firms practice independently and not in a relationship for the joint practice of law

Asset Protection Services of America

Helpful Definitions

AssetProtectionServices.com

Authorized Capital

Authorized capital is a notional amount of capital that a company is allowed to draw from its shareholders in consideration for the company shares. At the time of incorporation, the number of shares *authorized* will greatly exceed the number of shares *issued*. Any amount of authorized capital, as determined by the beneficial owners, may be stated in the company formation documents. There are no mandatory time frames as to when such capital must be paid up by the shareholders. Changes in capital stock may occur only with the approval of the company shareholders.

Confidentiality and Privacy

Information on the shareholders, directors and beneficial owners are not part of any public record. Only in keeping with formation "Due Diligence Information" requirements is a licensed registered agent permitted to privately possess internal company files. Such documents include the register of shareholders and directors and the company minutes and resolutions, but do not contain any indication as to the actual beneficial owners. The only documents on public file are the Memorandum and Articles of Association which do not contain any information on the actual company shareholders, directors or beneficial owners. Offshore resident agent laws impose a duty on professionals and can impose sentences of up to one year in prison and up to $50,000 in fines to keep the affairs of their clients strictly confidential and unaccessible to the public.

Confiscation Provisions

Where any foreign government authority, by way of nationalism, expropriation, confiscation, force or duress or similar action; or by imposition of any confiscatory tax, assessment, or other governmental charge, takes or seizes any shares or other interest of any offshore company, they may apply to the court for a decision ordering the company to disregard the attempted seizure and continue to respect the rights of the company owners.

Due Diligence Information

International Money Laundering Acts and Know Your Client (KYC) regulations impose Due Diligence Information (DDI) obligations upon all financial intermediaries requiring evidence of identity, residency and source of funds prior to entering into a business relationship. All international orders are required by law to provide complete and current Due Diligence Information.

Financial Reporting

Unless indicated, offshore companies are not required to prepare or file any financial accounts and are free to arrange their business accounts in any manner fitting to establish and maintain reasonable accuracy of the company's financial position.

Memorandum and Articles of Incorporation

The memorandum specifies the company name, location of the registered office, business activities, liabilities of the members and value of the company shares. The articles of association detail the issuance of shares, voting rights and dividend rights of shareholders, rules and meetings of the Board of Directors, and restrictions on the transfer of shares.

Name Restrictions

Names may not be used which are similar or identical to an existing company, a name which constitutes a criminal offense, is offensive, contrary to the public interest or implies royal or governmental patronage.

What is a Nominee?

A person (individual or corporate body) nominated and appointed to act in a public capacity on behalf of an officer, account signatory, or shareholder of a company in order to protect the identity and privacy of the true owners.

Nominee Director

A nominee director does not exist internationally in the same manner as in the United States. The person (individual or corporate body) listed as the director of a company is recognized by courts as the liable party for the proper administration of the company. Director services are accompanied with a signed fiduciary agreement binding the director to act only upon clear instruction from the shareholder(s) and, in addition to providing some anonymity, prevents unauthorized activities.

Nominee Shareholder

A person (individual or corporate body) nominated and appointed to be listed on applications and company documents in order to protect the identity and privacy of the actual owner. Shareholder services are accompanied with a signed declaration of trust binding the nominee shareholder to act only upon clear instruction from the actual owner and, in addition to providing some anonymity, prevents the unauthorized sale of shares.

Paid Up Capital

The amount of funding that has been paid in full for company shares. Most offshore companies are not required to have any minimum paid-up capital in order to initiate business operations.

Resident Agent and Registered Office

The resident agent is a licensed person (individual or corporate body) designated to receive service of process, summons and complaint (lawsuit), or vital government documents on behalf of an entity. The registered office is the physical location where an entity is domiciled and considered the physical point of contact for all official correspondence. A resident agent and registered office are mandatory in virtually every jurisdiction in the world.

Share Capital

The (currency specific) value of issued shares in a company. Not all jurisdictions require share capital to be fully paid at the time of incorporation. Generally, a company is incorporated with the highest allowable share capital at the lowest available government fee.

Shelf Company

A pre-existing company which remains in good standing and is sitting on a proverbial shelf available for purchase.

Structuring

Offshore companies have an independent legal personality and possesses the same powers as a natural person. A Company shareholder and director may be the same person and apart from the director, no other officers need be appointed. A current register (complete contact information) of shareholders and directors must be kept at the office of the local resident agent.

Ultimate Beneficial Owner (UBO)

The individual who enjoys the benefit of ownership in a company, even if title is held in the name of another nominee or person (individual or corporate body).

Asset Protection Services of America

Frequently Asked Questions

AssetProtectionServices.com

If I have insurance, do I still need asset protection?

Insurance policies are often mandatory and helpful in recovering your assets due to various types of loss. Be wary that not all insurance policies are alike and exclusions or claim denials could leave you without coverage. Insurance without proper entity structuring is no better than proper entity structuring without insurance. We recommend a sensible balance of both.

Which is more important, asset protection or tax savings?

Assets within an estate may vary in equity, cash flow, risk and overall sentimental value and should be weighed individually. If the benefits of asset protection work favorably with tax laws a person is fortunate and receive the best of both worlds, but other times the two may be diametrically opposed and a person is forced with compromising or choosing between the two.

Will my offshore company need to pay any taxes?

Most offshore companies pay very little, if any, taxes. St. Kitts and Nevis is a low-tax (0% tax) jurisdiction. So it is possible that your company many not be subject to any taxation whatsoever, but that is a question you would need to ask a competent tax advisor in your resident country as some nations (i.e. the United States) tax their citizens on worldwide income regardless of their residency status. Since laws, rules, rulings, regulations, statutes and codes are constantly changing and evolving, we recommend that you seek professional tax advice in your country of residence to establish any specific tax liabilities in your home jurisdiction.

Can offshore countries offer true privacy and confidentiality?

Yes they can. For example, the Republic of Seychelles is an independent nation and offers true privacy and confidentiality as they have avoided entering any information sharing agreements with other countries in exchange for foreign aid. Unless a person is wanted for serious international crimes such as drug smuggling, or is being investigated by the Financial Intelligence Unit for money laundering or INTERPOL suspects them for human trafficking, the Republic of Seychelles does not share or report any information to overseas 'principles' or organizations. Seychelles law regarding secrecy impose a duty on professionals to keep the affairs of their clients strictly confidential.

Why are resident agent and registered office services required?

Virtually every jurisdiction worldwide has a law which requires all business entities to retain a resident agent and registered office for the service of process. In the event that your entity was ever sued, the lawsuit would be delivered to the registered office of your resident agent who, in-turn, would have that paperwork couriered directly to you. The resident agent is required to have on file the name and contact information of the person who retains the ownership record ledger of the entity (even though the resident agent is not required to possess the ledger itself) in order to know where to mail such service of process. Each entity is provided resident agent and registered office services for a period of one year and is thereafter annually renewable.

Do I need virtual office services?

As tax collecting agents become more proficient in tax collection, it is helpful to demonstrate that your offshore entity meets the requisites of doing business internationally. Such proof may require a physical office staffed with well-trained personnel to provide your company with a base of operations in answering company telephone calls, receiving company mail, and sending invoices to clients.

Such additional company services can be retained at varying costs (where available) and may include:
-> A professional business location, which may be used as your mailing address on business cards, letterheads, invoices, websites and advertisements.
-> Telephone answering services, which may take messages for business calls on behalf of your entity in a professional manner during regular business hours.
-> Mail forwarding services, which may forward mail and packages to you anywhere worldwide and send out customized invoices to your clients.
Such full office services can be conveniently incorporated into your annual renewal fees.

How did you arrive at your current pricing structure and annual renewal rates?

Our prices for company formations, renewal fees and legal services are exactly the same as our legal provider in every jurisdiction. Fees for the respective law firms are commensurate to the work being performed. APSI consulting services are inclusive within our existing legal service provider fees. There are absolutely no price increases whatsoever for our consulting services.

How do I know when to complete my estate planning?

Asset protection is akin to wearing a seat belt. The decision to protect yourself, family and loved ones is made long before an accident occurs. Should you find yourself in the uncomfortable position where an accident is imminent, you simply cannot reach back and try to put your seat belt on and install an airbag during the split second before impact. In the same manner, once you have been served with a lawsuit, or should your family suffer the loss of your untimely death, your entire estate is effectively frozen. You either have your assets protected and your estate in order, or you don't. The best time to complete your estate planning is now!

Do you offer private consultations?

Yes. Please contact us today to schedule your private consultation.

Belize

AssetProtectionServices.com

About Belize

Activities

Belize is an outdoor enthusiast's playground with snorkeling, scuba diving, surfing, wind sailing, kayaking, canoeing, biking, hiking, cave exploring, river tubing, white-water rafting, jungle expeditions, fishing, bird watching, deep mountain forest camping and more. The Belize Barrier Reef has been named one of the "Seven Wonders of the Underwater World" by CEDAM International and Belize is home to ancient Mayan temples as well as some of the most exotic plant, animal and tree species on the planet.

Climate

Belize has a tropical Caribbean climate that is warm, humid and controlled in large part by the Atlantic trade winds. Along the coastline, temperatures average around 22°C in January and 25°C in July. As the trade winds loose strength moving inland, the mainland areas will see summer temperatures in excess of 38°C. The dry season is the most attractive time of year for tourists and generally runs from December through May. The rainy season extends from June through November and brings varying amounts of precipitation. The Corozal District in the north may only see 50 cm of rain, while Punta Gorda to the south may see in excess of 170 cm per annum. Notwithstanding the heavy wind, rain and flooding from a passing hurricane, Belize has consistent weather patterns.

Culture

Belize is the most sparsely populated country in Central America. Despite a majority of the citizenry being 18 years of age or younger, Belize possesses an impressive 94% literacy rate. The country is multi-cultural with resident ethnic groups such as the Mestizo, Creole, Mayan, Caribe and Garifuna. Belizians have one of the highest birth rates in the worlds, with an average of four children per family and a life expectancy of 68.3 years. The predominant religion in Belize is Christianity with Roman Catholics and Protestants making up the two primary denominations. Belize is unique in Central and South America in that English is the official language. This fact makes international business and tourism favorable for attracting many Americans, Canadians and Europeans to Belize.

Economy and Offshore Financial Services

Belize is a member of the British Commonwealth, United Nations, WTO, IMF and other international organizations. The Queen of England is the head of state and formally represented in Belize by the Governor General. The national assembly, comprised of the house of representatives and the senate, carries out the duties of the legislative branch of the Belizian parliamentary democracy. The executive branch is overseen by the government and the prime minister. Belize is divided into 6 administrative districts; Belize, Cayo, Corozal, Orange Walk, Stan Creek and Toledo. Belize is known for its exports of tropical agrarian products including bananas, citrus, fish, sugar and timber. Belize has a very long 6 month tourist season attracting hundreds of thousands of people from around the world. The Belize International Business Companies Act in 1990 has steadily given rise to a strong financial offshore services economy. When Belize refused to cower to unjust pressure by the United States to reveal confidential client information, they eventually were exonerated after years of international isolation as a respected member of the offshore financial services community. The primary commercial banks in Belize are the Alliance Bank, Atlantic Bank, Bank of Nova Scotia, Belize Bank and the First Caribbean International Bank. Asset Protection Services of America offers incorporation services for International Business Companies in Belize.

Geography

Belize is the northern most country in Central America. Located along the southeast part of the Yucatan peninsula, the entire east coast of Belize faces the Caribbean Sea. Belize is a seaside country spanning 280 kilometers from north to south and 105 kilometers from east to west. Much of the Hondo river creates a natural borderline between Belize and Mexico to the north and Guatemala to the west and south. The highest point in Belize is Victoria Peak standing 1,120 meters above sea level in the Maya Mountains. The Belize River, also known as the Old River, is the nation's largest and most historic waterway. Navigable up to the Guatemalan border, the Belize River allows for goods and services to be transported deep inland and gave rise to the name of Belize City, which is situated near the mouth of the trade route. Over 90% of Belize is saturated with virgin tropical rain forests,

rich in flora, fauna and precious species of timber. Belize boasts hundreds of picturesque islands, islets, cayes, a 322 kilometer barrier reef (largest in the northern hemisphere and second largest in the world) and the biggest sinkhole on earth, Blue Hole.

History

The ancient Mayan civilization inhabited Belize for centuries with a population at one point believed to exceed 400,000 people. Europeans came to know of modern day Belize City with the discovery by Christopher Columbus in 1502. Due to the resilience of the inland natives, it wasn't until 1786 that the British government was able to appoint a Quartermaster General representative to Belize for the first time. In 1862 Belize was officially declared a British Colony and was renamed "British Honduras" and continued under this name for more than 100 years. When the demand for internationally exported timber diminished in the twentieth century Belizians rose up and gained their independence as a nation in 1964. In 1973 the country renamed itself Belize and in 1980 the United Nations adopted a resolution recognizing Belize as an independent sovereign nation.

Interesting Facts

Capital
Belmopan

Population
333,200

Official Language
English

GDP
$2.651 Billion

Government
British Commonwealth
Parliamentary Democracy
Constitutional Monarchy

Currency
Belize Dollar (BZD)

Laws
Common Law

Driving
Right

Independence Day
September 21st, 1981

Internet
.bz

Total Area
22,966 Km2

Calling Code
+501

Belize
International Business Company (IBC)

Introduction

A Belize International Business Company (IBC) is a tax-free company designed to engage in international business transactions with strict owner privacy laws, minimal record keeping and no reporting requirements. Since the introduction of the Belize International Business Companies Act in 1990 (Amended in 2000), tens of thousands of IBC's have been formed and registered. Belize is heavily invested into its incorporation services industry with a modern computerized IBC Registry capable of processing a company registration within an hour. An International Business Company is suited for management consultants, network engineers, software developers, professionals who tend to travel between various countries on short-term assignments, internet based businesses, international commodity trading, investors and financial transaction businesses. A Belize IBC may be used as a personal asset protection vehicle to passively hold property and investments.

<u>Belize</u>   <u>International Business Company</u>

Company Laws	International Business Companies Act, 2000
Official Document Language	English
Conduct Business Internationally	Yes
Conduct Business in Belize	No
Resident Agent Required	Yes
Registered Office Required	Yes
Resident Secretary Required	No
Company Taxation	0 % of Worldwide Income
Double Taxation Avoidance Agreements	No
Company Tax Resident Qualification	No
Income Tax and Business Tax	No
Detailed Client Application Required	No
Minimum Shareholders	1
Company Shareholders Allowed	Yes
Residency of Shareholders Allowed	Any Nationality
Register of Shareholders	In Private Possession of Registered Agent
Register of Shareholders Public Record	No
Bearer Shares Permitted	Yes *(Only in Possession of Registered Agent)*
Minimum Directors	1
Company Directors Allowed	Yes
Residency of Directors Allowed	Any Nationality
Register of Directors	In Private Possession of Registered Agent
Register of Directors Public Record	No
Disclosure of Beneficial Owners to Reg. Agent	Yes *(Due Diligence Requirements)*
Disclosure of Beneficial Owners with Registrar	No
Annual General Meeting Required	No
Shareholders / Directors Meeting Required	Yes *(Anywhere in the World or by Proxy)*
Company Minutes and Resolutions	In Private Possession of Registered Agent
Company Seal Required	Yes
Minimum Paid Up Capital Required	No
Maximum Authorized Capital Investment	Unlimited *(Fees in Excess of 50,000 Shares)*
Capital Considerations	Any Currency or in Kind
Subject to Currency Controls and Restrictions	No
Application Fees	No
Annual Government Fees	$100 *(Under $50,000 Authorized Capital)*
	$1,000 *(Over $50,000 Authorized Capital)*
	$350 *(Issuance of Any No Par Value Stock)*
Keeping of Accounts Required	No
Filing of Accounts and Returns Required	No
Annual Government Return Filing Fees	No
Auditing of Accounts Required	No
Re-Domicile from a Foreign Country	Yes
Re-Domicile to a Foreign Country	Yes
Shelf Companies Available	Yes
Incorporation Time	1 Business Day

Confidentiality and Privacy

In 1996, the United States of America tried to pressure the sovereign nation of Belize into signing the Mutual Legal Assistance Treaty (MLAT). Belize refused as such a treaty would allow for the exchange of confidential information, such as bank records and other sensitive information, based on a broad range of requests including tax investigations.

Belize did sign a limited Legal Assistance Treaty with the U.S. where client information would only be disclosed under internationally recognized grievous crimes such as drug trading, terrorism and human trafficking. At the time, Belize was wrongfully accused of harboring money-launderers and was "blacklisted" by the United States of America, suffering unjust restrictions of foreign aid, world political isolation and an economic crisis.

Belize would not give in to such tactics and by upholding their commitments to the banking "know your client" regulations, Belize was eventually exonerated. By standing their ground to the world's super-power, Belize has emerged as a credible and secure offshore asset protection and tax haven

Government Licensing Fees

The annual government licensing fees in Belize are $100 provided the authorized capital is under $50,000. If the authorized capital exceeds $50,000 then the annual government licensing fee is $1,000. Should any "no par value" stocks be issued the annual government licensing fee is $350.

Name Endings

AS	Aktiengesellschaft
AS	Sociedad Anomina
Corp	Corporation
Inc	Incorporated
Ltd	Limited
SA	Société Anonyme

Rules of Operation

Belize International Business Companies Act, 2000
Part II - Constitution of Companies (Section 5(1))

(1) *For the purposes of this Act, an International Business Company is a company that does not:*

(a) *carry on business with persons resident in Belize;*

(b) *own an interest in real property situate in Belize, other than a lease referred to in paragraph (e) of subsection (2);*

(c) *carry on a banking business unless it is licensed under an enactment authorizing it to carry on such business;*

(d) *carry on business as an insurance or a reinsurance company, insurance agent or insurance broker, unless it is licensed under an enactment authorizing it carry on such business;*

(e) *carry on the business of providing the registered office for companies,*

(f) *carry on trust business, unless it is licensed under an enactment authorizing it carry on such business;*

(g) *carry on collective investment schemes, unless it is licensed under an enactment authorizing it carry on such business;*

(h) *hold shares, stock, debt obligations or other securities in a company incorporated under the Companies Act or under any enactment amending or substituting the Act;*

(i) *subject to subsection (4) below, issue its shares, stock, debt obligations or other securities to any person resident in Belize or to any company incorporated under the Companies Act or under any enactment amending or substituting the said Act.*

Shares

A Belize IBC may issue registered shares or bearer shares and may be designated as:

1.) Bearer
2.) Common
3.) No Par Value
4.) Non-Voting
5.) Preferred
6.) Redeemable
7.) Unnumbered
8.) Voting
9.) Shares having more or less than one vote per share
10.) Shares that may be voted only when held by persons who meet specified requirements
11.) Shares that entitle participation only on certain assets
12.) Shares that may be voted only on certain matters
13.) Shares that may be voted only upon the occurrence of certain events

Bearer Shares

Bearer shares must remain in the private physical possession of a licensed Registered Agent in Belize.

Taxation

By legal definition, a Belize IBC and its shareholders are not subject to any tax derived from any income on all dividends, distributions, interest, rent, royalties, compensations, transfers of property, transactions of shares, debt obligations and other securities by persons who are not residents of Belize.

Belize International Business Companies Act, 2000
Chapter 270
Part XII - Exemptions from Tax
Section 130 - Exemptions from tax, etc.

(1) *Notwithstanding any provision of the Income and Business Tax Act, but subject to the provisions of this section -*

(a) *all income of a company incorporated under this Act . . .*
(b) *all dividends or other distributions paid by the company to persons who are not resident in Belize;*
(c) *all interest, rent, royalties, compensations and other amounts paid by the company to persons who are not persons resident in Belize; and*
(d) *capital gains realized with respect to any shares, debt obligations or other securities of a company incorporated under this Act by persons who are not persons resident in Belize,*

are exempt from all provisions of the Income and Business Tax Act.

(2) *Notwithstanding any provision of the Stamp Duties Act, but subject to the provisions of this section:-*

(a) *all instruments relating to transfers of any property to a company incorporated under this Act;*
(b) *all instruments relating to transactions in respect of the shares, debt obligations or other securities of a company incorporated under this Act; and*
(c) *all instruments relating in any way to the assets or activities of a company incorporated under this Act,*

are exempt from the payment of stamp duty.

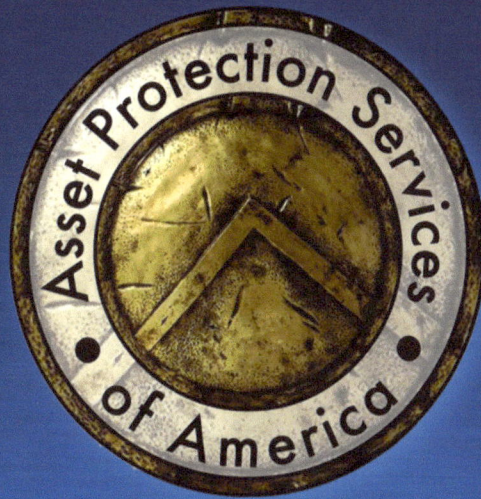

British Virgin Islands

About the British Virgin Islands

Activities

'The deep port in Road Town permits some of the largest commercial luxury liners to dock impressively close to land. Year-round snorkeling and scuba diving entices tourists to take spontaneous excursions to the BVI beaches. Catamarans, sail boats and yachts are all available for private charter. At 29 kilometers in length, the Horseshoe Reef on Anegada Island is the largest barrier coral reef in the Caribbean Sea and 4th largest in the world. The Baths at Virgin Gorda Island are a famous natural attraction with warm, shallow waters among enormous granite rocks. Sporting activities such as golf, tennis, wind-surfing, para-sailing and jet-skiing are plentiful. Local boutiques are open for late afternoon or evening shopping and regional chefs serve a variety of Caribbean dishes and fine european wines.

Climate

The British Virgin Islands enjoy a balmy tropical climate with temperate weather patterns moderated by easterly trade winds. The BVI do not experience four distinct seasons, but rather a long summer and mild winter with only a two hour deviation in sunlight between the solstices. The temperature averages around 28°C and varies little throughout the year as winters rarely go below 25°C and summers don't often exceed 32°C. Annual rainfall measures around 1 meter with two-thirds falling during the months of September through November. Hurricanes may occasionally reach the islands bringing heavy rains and rough seas, but may only make landfall on one or two occasions in a person's lifetime.

Culture

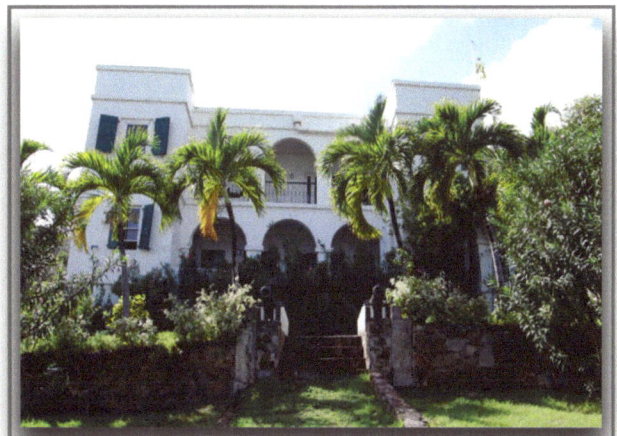

The ancestry of British Virgin Islanders can be traced to West Africa including Nigeria, Senegal, the Congo's, Gambia and Ghana; from Europe in Denmark, the Netherlands and France as well as some North American influence. Its common for natives to "island hop" and trace their family heritage throughout the Caribbean. Much of the foods are imported and tend to be served spicy. "Fungi" is a staple diet in the BVI comprised of boiled cornmeal and okra cooked to a thick consistency. Interestingly, Fungi is also the name given to a regional style of music improvisation using washboards. Traditional island "quadrille" dancing is common alongside the meringue and salsa. Soccer and cricket are popular sports played regularly.

Economy and Offshore Financial Services

The British Virgin Islands has one of the most stable and prosperous economies in the Caribbean. Although the BVI export some commodities like rum, fresh fish, fruits, animals, gravel and sand, the twin pillars of the economy are tourism and financial services. Tourism accounts for 45% of the national income supporting a multitude of local businesses owners and their employees. Nearly 1 Million tourists vacation in the British Virgin Islands annually, half of which arrive on cruise ships.

Licensing fees for offshore business companies account for 52% of government revenues. There are more than 500,000 "active" companies currently registered in the BVI. The Financial Services Commission (FSC) is the regulatory authority for financial services business operating in and from within the BVI. According to the Foreign & Commonwealth Office, "Problems associated with drug trafficking are potentially the most serious threat to stability in the BVI." However, the United Kingdom National Audit Office reported that it is better equipped through its Financial Investigation Agency to investigate financial crime in the BVI than many other offshore centers. The BVI offshore industry is compliant with the Organization for Economic Cooperation and Development (OECD), the Financial Action Task Force (FATF) and the International Monetary Fund (IMF). Asset Protection Services of America offers incorporation services for Business Companies in the British Virgin Islands.

Geography

The British Virgin Islands are in the Caribbean Sea, east of Puerto Rico and adjacent to the U.S. Virgin Islands. Tortola, the largest of the British Virgin Islands, spans 20 kilometers in length by 5 kilometers in width and is home to 21,000 people out of an overall population of 25,000. Of the nearly 60 small islands, cays and islets, roughly 15 of the islands are inhabited, such as Jost Van Dyke, Virgin Gorda and Anegada. Most of the islands are volcanic in origin and have characteristically rugged terrain. Anegada is geologically distinct from the other BVI islands in that it is composed of limestone and coral. With less than 200 inhabitants, Anegada is incredibly flat with the highest elevation reaching a mere 8.5 meters above sea level.

History

The British Virgin Islands are believed to have been inhabited by Amerindians as far back as 1,500 B.C. The South American Arawak were credited with the first settlements around 100 B.C. where they lived until the Caribs from the Lesser Antilles Islands displaced them sometime in 500 A.D. The aggressive nature of the Caribs earned such a reputation as to have the Caribbean Sea named after them. Christopher Columbus was the first european explorer to have sighted the islands In 1493. The formal name he gave to the islands was "Santa Ursula las Once Mil Virgenes" meaning, "Saint Ursula and Her 11,000 Virgins". It was later shortened to "Las Virgenes" or "The Virgins". For almost 200 years the English, Dutch, French, Danish and pirates fought for ownership of the islands until England gained control with the capture of Tortola in 1672. The (British) Virgin Islands were then used as a strategic military port for decades. The English planted sugar cane fields and forced African slave labor to harvest the crops on plantations until the Slave Abolition Act in 1833. It wasn't until 1967 that the islands gained their autonomy, retaining the status of a British Overseas Territory with a local "Premier" to oversee foreign affairs and economic issues.

Interesting Facts

Capital
Road Town

Population
27,000

Official Language
English

GDP
$1.6 Billion

Government
British Overseas Territory

Currency
United States Dollar

Laws
Common Law

Driving
Left

Independence Day
1967

Internet
.vg

Total Area
153 Km2

Calling Code
+1 (284)

British Virgin Islands
Business Company

Introduction

Business Companies formed in the British Virgin Islands are renowned worldwide as the staple offshore incorporation destination. In 2000, the British government commissioned KPMG (one of the world's largest professional services and auditing firms) to produce a report on the offshore financial services industry. It was determined that nearly 41% of the world's offshore tax-exempt international business companies had been formed in the British Virgin Islands. Since 1984 over 600,000 incorporations have been amassed by business owners, entrepreneurs and investors choosing the BVI as their base of operations. The new BVI Business Companies Act 2004 was passed and came into effect on January 1, 2005. This legislation now regulates the registration, status and operation of newly formed business companies and all former international business companies (also known as BVI's). The new Act addresses the discriminatory pressures inherent between domestic BVI companies and offshore BVI international business companies. Previously BVI's were restricted to international transactions whereas now any distinction between local and offshore companies has been removed. According to the new legislation there is one unified company, a BVI Business Company. This Act has replaced and superseded the BVI International Business Companies Act of 1984 and enhanced the appeal of incorporating in the British Virgin Islands as evidenced by over 5,000 new private entities created monthly.

British Virgin Islands   Business Company

Company Laws	Business Companies Act, 2004
Official Document Language	English
Conduct Business Internationally	Yes
Conduct Business in British Virgin Islands	Yes
Resident Agent Required	Yes
Registered Office Required	Yes
Resident Secretary Required	No
Company Taxation	0 % of Worldwide Income
Double Taxation Avoidance Agreements	Yes
Company Tax Resident Qualification	Yes
Income Tax and Business Tax	None
Detailed Client Application Required	No
Minimum Shareholders	1
Company Shareholders Allowed	Yes
Residency of Shareholders Allowed	Any Nationality
Register of Shareholders	In Private Possession of Registered Agent
Register of Shareholders Public Record	No
Bearer Shares Permitted	Yes (Held by licensed custodian in BVI)
Minimum Directors	1
Company Directors Allowed	Yes
Residency of Directors Allowed	Any Nationality
Register of Directors	In Private Possession of Registered Agent
Register of Directors Public Record	No
Disclosure of Beneficial Owners to Reg. Agent	Yes (Due Diligence Requirements)
Disclosure of Beneficial Owners with Registrar	No
Annual General Meeting Required	No
Shareholders / Directors Meeting Required	Yes (Anywhere in the World or by Proxy)
Company Minutes and Resolutions	In Private Possession of Registered Agent
Company Seal Required	Yes (Imprint kept with Registered Agent)
Minimum Paid Up Capital Required	None
Maximum Authorized Capital Investment	Unlimited (Fees in Excess of 50,000 Shares)
Capital Considerations	Any Currency or in Kind
Subject to Currency Controls and Restrictions	No
Application Fees	No
Annual Government Fees	$350
Filing of Accounts and Returns Required	No
Annual Government Return Filing Fees	None
Auditing of Accounts Required	No
Re-Domicile from a Foreign Country	Yes
Re-Domicile to a Foreign Country	Yes
Shelf Companies Available	Yes
Incorporation Time	1 Business Day

Incorporating Offshore *(2nd Edition)*
by Jay Butler

Financial Reporting

A BVI Business Company is not required to prepare or file any financial accounts. However, if nominee director services are provided, the company must keep records that are sufficient to "show and explain" the company's transactions within reasonable accuracy to the Director (also known as a BVI Compliance Officer) upon request at any time.

British Virgin Islands Business Companies Act, 2004
Part V - Company Administration
Division 2 - Company records
Section 98 - Financial Records

(1) A company shall keep records that
    (a)   are sufficient to show and explain the company's transactions; and
    (b)   will, at any time, enable the financial position of the company to be determined with reasonable accuracy.

(2) A company that contravenes this section commits an offense and is liable on summary conviction to a fine of $10,000 (USD).

Government Licensing Fees

A complete list of all business company fees can be found under Schedule 1 (on page 153) of the BVI Business Companies Act. Otherwise, in general, the annual renewal fee for a BVI Business Company is a competitive $350 (USD).

Name Endings

Corp	Corporation
Inc	Incorporated
Ltd	Limited
SA	Société Anonyme or Sociedad Anomina
SPC	Segregated Portfolio Company
(SPV) Ltd	Restricted Purpose
(SPV) SPC	Restricted Purpose, Segregated Portfolio Company
Unltd	Unlimited

Page 36 of 127
© 2004 - 2016 Asset Protection Services of America. All Rights Reserved. AssetProtectionServices.com

Name Restrictions

British Virgin Islands Business Companies Act, 2004
Part II - Incorporation, Capacity and Powers
Division 3 - Company Names
Section 18 - Restrictions on Company Names

(1) No company shall be registered, whether or incorporation, continuation, merger or consolidation under a name

(a)   the use of which would contravene another enactment or the regulations;

(b)   that, subject to section 24,

  (i)   is identical to the name under which a company is or has been registered under this Act or a former Act, or

  (ii)   is so similar to the name under which a company is or has been registered under this Act or a former Act that the use of the name would, in the opinion of the Registrar, be likely to confuse or mislead;

(c)   that is identical to a name that has been reserved under section 25 or that is so similar to a name that has been reserved under section 25 that the use of both names by different companies would, in the opinion of the Registrar, be likely to confuse or mislead;

(d)   that contains a restricted word or phrase, unless the Commission has given its prior written consent to the use of the word or phrase; or

(e)   that, in the opinion of the Registrar, is offensive or, for any other reason, objectionable.

Rules of Operation

British Virgin Islands Business Companies Act, 2004
Part II - Incorporation, Capacity and Powers
Division 4 - Capacity and Powers
Section 28 - Capacity and Powers

(1) Subject to this Act, any other enactment and its memorandum and articles, a company has, irrespective of corporate benefit,

(a)   full capacity to carry on or undertake any business or activity, do any act or enter into any transaction;

Shares

A BVI Business Company may issue registered shares or bearer shares. All issued shares must be paid up in full. Company shares may be designated as:

1.) Bearer

2.) Common

3.) No Par Value

4.) Non-Voting

5.) Preferred

6.) Redeemable

7.) Voting

8.) Shares having more or less than one vote per share

9.) Shares that may be voted only when held by persons who meet specified requirements

10.) Shares that entitle participation only on certain assets

11.) Shares that may be voted only on certain matters

12.) Shares that may be voted only upon the occurrence of certain events

Note: See BVI Business Company Act, Part III - Shares, Division 1 - General

Bearer Shares

The British Virgin Islands permit the issuance of bearer shares. However, the bearer shares must remain in the possession of a licensed custodian in BVI. Should the bearer shares remain in the possession of a custodian located outside BVI then a $750 fee is applied and written disclosure of the actual beneficial owners must be revealed, which largely negates the benefit.

Taxation

By legal definition, a BVI Business Company is exempt from all provisions of the Income Tax Ordinance, notwithstanding transactions relating to property in the Virgin Islands.

British Virgin Islands Business Companies Act, 2004
Part XIV - Administration and General
Section 242 - Exemptions from Tax

(1) *Notwithstanding any provisions of the Income Tax Ordinance*
   (a) *a company,*
   (b) *all dividends, interests, rents, royalties, compensations and other amounts paid by a company, and*
   (c) *capital gains realized with respect to any shares, debt obligations or other securities of a company, are exempt from all provisions of the Income Tax Ordinance.*

(2) *No estate, inheritance, succession or gift tax is payable with respect to any shares, debt obligations or other securities of a company.*

(3) *Subject to subsection(4), notwithstanding any provision of the Stamp Act,*
   (a) *all instruments relating to transfers of property to or by a company,*
   (b) *all instruments relating to transactions in respect of the shares, debt obligations or other securities of a company, and*
   (c) *all instruments relating to other transactions relating to the business of a company, are exempt from payment of stamp duty.*

(4) *Subsection (3) does not apply to an instrument relating to*
   (a) *the transfer to or by a company of an interest in land situated in the Virgin Islands; or*
   (b) *transactions in respect of the shares, debt obligations or other securities of a land owning company.*

(5) *For the purposes of subsection (4), a company is a land owning company if it, or any of its subsidiaries, has an interest in any land in the Virgin Islands.*

(6) *Notwithstanding any provisions of the Registration and Records Act, all deeds and other instruments relating to*
   (a) *transfers of a property to or by a company*
   (b) *transactions in respect of the shares, debt obligations or other securities of a company,*
   (c) *other transactions relating to the business of a company, are exempt from the provisions of that Act.*

Double Taxation Avoidance Agreement (DTAA)

Japan
Switzerland

Tax Information Exchange Agreement (TIEA)

TIEA Signed and Ratified	TIEA Pending Ratification	TIEA Under Negotiation
Australia	Aruba	Czechoslovakia
Denmark	China	Slovenia
Faroe Islands	Netherlands	Canada
Finland	Netherlands Antilles	
France		
Germany		
Greenland		
Iceland		
Ireland		
New Zealand		
Norway		
Portugal		
Sweden		
United Kingdom		
United States		

European Union Savings Directive

The EU Savings Directive (2005) is aimed at the reporting of *personal bank accounts* held in other EU member states. The directive is intended to prevent account holders from avoiding paying taxes on interest, dividends and other income through offshore personal accounts. Legislation continues to be drafted encroaching on the privacy of company beneficial owners, trusts and foundations. However these laws are only applicable to EU countries and the participating nations of Anguilla, Aruba, BVI, Caymans, Cyprus, Barbados, Turks & Caicos, Jersey, Guernsey, Gibraltar and Isle of Man. If you are a resident within the European Union incorporating in the British Virgin Islands (BVI) and plan on opening a bank account in the BVI, then you should consult with your tax advisor regarding the EU Savings Directive.

Asset Protection Services of America

About Hong Kong

About Hong Kong

Activities

The number one tourist destination in Hong Kong is Victoria Peak, featuring the peak tram, galleria and tower. There is a 5.7 kilometer cable car ride up to the Big Buddha, an Ocean Amusement Park and even a Hong Kong Disneyland. Ferry rides, cruise ships and helicopter flights offer city tours. The Museum of Art, Museum of History and Philharmonic Orchestra are located downtown. Street markets contain local venders to high-end shopping centers with luxury items providing access to an array of shopping experiences. Hong Kong is a metropolitan wonderland with top hotels from around the world, service oriented day spas and restaurants with cuisine from every corner of the earth.

Climate

Hong Kong has a subtropical climate averaging 23°C with 78% humidity. Monsoons are common along with the seasonal alternation of winds. January is the coldest month dropping down to 10°C or lower on occasion. Spring lasts from March through the middle of May bringing heavy rains and very little sunshine. The transition from winter to spring is considered the most undesirable time of year, even miserable with nearly 2 meters of rainfall. The summer months have intense sunshine running from June through the middle of September and are characteristically hot and humid reaching temperatures of 33°C with 86% humidity. The fall season and first half of winter are dry, cool and considered the most pleasant time of year.

Culture

Although 95% of Hongkongese are of Chinese decent, Hong Kong is recognized as a hub of cultural diversity. Family surnames are traditionally listed first in honor of the father, followed by two personal names. Confucianism drives the system of ethics and relational responsibilities such as duty, loyalty and respect. Business cards are given using two hands, often with a slight bow and eyes lowered. The concept of "face" is an intangible quality representing dignity, reputation and prestige that is dynamically woven into the fabric of Asian society. Mainstream educational systems in Hong Kong place a heavy emphasis on ranking systems beginning at an early age as competition for job placement is fierce. Business relationships are developed carefully and are intended to be maintained for lengthy periods of time.

Economy

Hong Kong has the highest degree of autonomy as a Special Administrative Region of the People's Republic of China in all areas except defense and foreign affairs. Individual rights and freedoms are enshrined in the "Hong Kong Basic Law" constitution. The legal system is based on English common law and completely independent of China's civil law. The Hong Kong government is made of a Legislative Council, Executive Council, Judiciary and Civil Service. The Executive Council is headed by the Chief Executive, who is chosen by the Election Committee and appointed by the Central People's Government. The Political & Economic Risk Consultancy rated Hong Kong as the "2nd most politically stable country in Asia" with the "best Judicial system in Asia". A total of 70 out of the world's 100 largest banks have licensed representative offices in Hong Kong. The Stock Exchange of Hong Kong (SEHK) is the 6th largest in the world with over $2.3 Trillion (USD) in market capitalization. The Hong Kong government has few, if any, import and export regulations allowing the market to control the rate of development. The official government policy of "positive non-interventionism" is often cited as laissez-faire capitalism, the success of which can be seen with an unemployment rate just over 4%. Since Hong Kong has virtually no natural resources, 90% of the Gross Domestic Product is understandably driven by the service sector. The 2010 World Bank Report "Doing Business" rated Hong Kong the "World's #3 Easiest Place to do Business".

Geography

Hong Kong is located along the southern coast of China, about 160 kilometers southeast of Guanzhou, formerly Canton. The Hong Kong territories cover 1,100 square kilometers and contain more than 200 offshore islands, the largest of which is Lantau. Regionally situated between the Taiwan Straits, the South China Sea and the Pacific Ocean, the area is a strategic channel for international sea traffic. With mountainous regions to the North and South, accommodating deep harbors and territorial waters extending 5.6 kilometers from shore, Hong Kong is a favorable port renowned for its spectacular skyline.

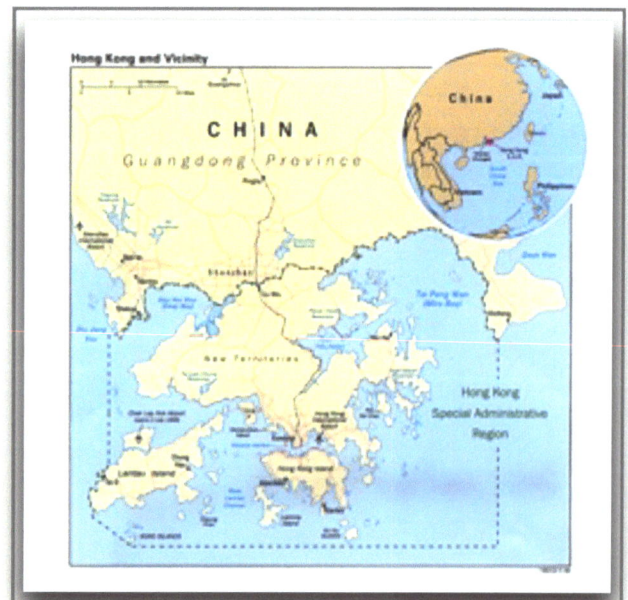

History

The history of Hong Kong extends back six millennium. The first emperor of China was recorded in 214 B.C. and formed imperial China. Chinese history is exhaustive as dynasties lasted for centuries. The earliest recorded european visitor was a Portuguese explorer who arrived in 1513. From 1661 to 1669, during a period of civil unrest, the territory was evacuated and largely became a wasteland. The East India Company was the first sea venture to China in 1699 and British merchant trading developed rapidly. Within a hundred years China was consuming over 2,000 chests of opium annually. When authorities refused to import more opium the first of two opium wars erupted and British forces occupied Hong Kong Island. In 1842 under the Treaty of Nanking, Hong Kong was ceded in perpetuity to the United Kingdom and a year later became a crown colony with the founding of the capital Victoria City. In the early 1950's when a city to the north of Hong Kong called Shenzhen became a "Special Economic Zone" of the People's Republic of China (PRC), Hong Kong was established as a center for foreign investments into China. When the United Kingdom reclassified Hong Kong as a "Dependent Territory" in 1983, discussions began to transfer sovereignty. And in 1984 the Sino-British Joint Declaration was signed stipulating that Hong Kong would be governed as a PRC "Special Administrative Region" retaining a high degree of autonomy for at least 50 years after the transfer. On July 1, 1997 the transfer of sovereignty occurred ending 156 years of British colonial rule. Hong Kong remains economically independent to this day.

Interesting Facts

Capital
Hong Kong

Population
7,100,000

Official Language
Chinese and English

GDP
$225 Billion

Government
Partial Democracy

Currency
Hong Kong Dollar (HKD)

Laws
Common Law

Driving
Left

Independence Day
July 1st, 1997

Internet
.hk

Total Area
1,078 Km2

Calling Code
+852

Hong Kong
Private Company Limited by Shares

Introduction

A Hong Kong Private Company Limited by Shares is recognized internationally as a "low tax" jurisdiction and a preferred vehicle for many European nationals. Provided no business is conducted with or within Hong Kong or by a Hong Kong resident, there are no Hong Kong tax liabilities. And utilizing a properly structured offshore entity as the shareholder of a Private Company Limited by Shares not only aids in enhancing anonymity and asset protection benefits, it can eliminate any tax liability for citizens outside Hong Kong who wish to have their business headquartered in Asia.

Hong Kong   Private Company Limited by Shares

Company Laws	Companies Ordinance, Chapter 32
Official Document Language	English and Chinese
Conduct Business Internationally	Yes
Conduct Business in Hong Kong	Yes
Resident Agent Required	No
Registered Office Required	Yes
Resident Secretary Required	Yes *(May be a Corporate Body)*
Company Taxation	0 % of Worldwide Income *(If **all** business is conducted outside H.K.)* 16.5% of Worldwide Income *(If **any** business is conducted inside H.K.)*
Double Taxation Avoidance Agreements	*No*
Company Tax Resident Qualification	Yes
Income Tax and Business Tax	Yes *(If business is conducted inside H.K.)*
Detailed Client Application Required	No
Minimum Shareholders	1 *(Must be 18 years of age or older)*
Company Shareholders Allowed	Yes
Residency of Shareholders Allowed	Any Nationality
Register of Shareholders	Filed with the Registry
Register of Shareholders Public Record	Yes
Bearer Shares Permitted	No
Minimum Directors	1 (Must be 18 years of age or older)
Company Directors Allowed	Yes
Residency of Directors Allowed	Any Nationality
Register of Directors	Filed with the Registry
Register of Directors Public Record	Yes
Disclosure of Beneficial Owners to Reg. Agent	Yes *(Due Diligence Requirements)*
Disclosure of Beneficial Owners with Registrar	No
Annual General Meeting Required	No
Shareholders / Directors Meeting Required	Yes *(Anywhere in the World or by Proxy)*
Company Minutes and Resolutions	In Private Possession of Registered Agent
Company Seal Required	Yes
Minimum Paid Up Capital Required	None
Maximum Authorized Capital Investment	Unlimited *(Fees in Excess of 50,000 Shares)*
Capital Considerations	Any Currency or in Kind
Subject to Currency Controls and Restrictions	No
Application Fees	No
Annual Government Fees	$315
Keeping / Filing Accounts & Returns Required	Yes
Annual Government Return Filing Fees	$15
Auditing of Accounts Required	Yes *(Within 18 Months, Annually Thereafter)*
Re-Domicile from a Foreign Country	Yes
Re-Domicile to a Foreign Country	Yes
Shelf Companies Available	Yes
Incorporation Time	7 to 10 Business Days

Confidentiality and Privacy

Information on shareholders and directors are sent to the Companies Registry and part of the public record. However, if nominee services are utilized then information on the beneficial owners remain private.

Economic Freedom

The Heritage Foundation "Index of Economic Freedom" continues to rate Hong Kong as the "World's #1 Freest Economy" as it has done for 29 consecutive years since the foundation's inception in 1985. Although the overall economic freedom score was 89.7 for the year 2010, out of 183 competing countries, Hong Kong is the only one to have ever achieved an over all score of 90 points or above out of 100. The Hong Kong Dollar is pegged to the United States Dollar at a permanent exchange rate of $7.75 (HKD) to $1.00 (USD).

Financial Reporting

A Hong Kong Private Company Limited by Shares is required to appoint a locally registered auditor who must be a member of the Hong Kong Society of Accountants (HKSA). Every HK company is required to be audited within 18 months of incorporation and annually thereafter. Accounts are not on public record, but are required by the Inland Revenue as are the keeping of books of account.

Hong Kong Companies Ordinance, Chapter 32
Part IV - Management and Administration
Section 121 - Keeping of Books of Account

(1) *Every company shall cause to be kept proper books of account with respect to-*
  (a) *all sums of money received and expanded by the company and the matters in respect of which the receipt and expenditure takes place;*
  (b) *all sales and purchases of goods by the company;*
  (c) *the assets and liabilities of the company.*

Government Licensing Fees

The annual business registration fee for a Hong Kong Private Company Limited by Shares is $2,450 (Hong Kong Dollars) or approximately $315 (United States Dollars).

Name Endings

Ltd	Limited

Name Restrictions

Hong Kong Private Company Limited by Shares may not be similar or identical to an existing company, a name which constitutes a criminal offense, is offensive, contrary to the public interest or implies royal or governmental patronage.

Rules of Operation

Hong Kong Companies Ordinance, Chapter 32
Part I - Incorporation of Companies and Matters Incidental Thereto
Section 5A - Powers of a Company

(1) A company has the capacity and the rights, powers and privileges of a natural person.

(2) Without limiting subsection (1), a company may do anything which it is permitted or required to do by its memorandum or by any enactment or rule of law.

Shares

Company shares may be designated as:

1.) Voting   **3.)** Ordinary   **5.)** Redeemable
2.) Non-Voting   **4.)** Preferred

Bearer Shares

"Bearer" shares and "no par value" shares are strictly prohibited.

Structuring

A Hong Kong Private Company Limited by Shares has an independent legal personality and possesses the same powers as a natural person. A Company shareholder and director may be the same person and a resident secretary is required. A current register (complete contact information) of shareholders and directors must be kept on-file at the local office.

Taxation

0% Tax on Worldwide Income
(If all business is conducted outside Hong Kong)

A Hong Kong Private Company Limited by Shares has no capital gains tax, no Value Added Tax (VAT), no Goods and Services Tax (GST), no estate duty, no withholding tax on dividends or interest and is not subject to the European Union savings tax directive. Provided *all* company income derived from from abroad, it is free from tax liabilities in Hong Kong.

16.5% Tax on Worldwide Income
(If any business is conducted inside Hong Kong)

Should a Hong Kong Private Company Limited by Shares conduct *any* business whatsoever with or within Hong Kong or by a Hong Kong resident, the worldwide income of that company will be subject to a 16.5% corporate tax.

Republic of Seychelles

About the Republic of Seychelles

Activities

Seychelles holds the record of any nation as having the highest percentage of land under natural conservation. Nearly 50% of the total land area in Seychelles is a natural wildlife reserve. Environmental legislation is incredibly strict as every tourism project undergoes an environmental review, including lengthy consultations with the public & conservationists. The end result of such coordinated development has lead Seychelles to be a world leader in sustainable tourism. Seychelles maintains an intact and stable environment and since 1993 guarantees its citizenry the right to a clean environment under law. Seychelles proudly offers some of the cleanest beaches and finest aquatic activities in the world. With over 1,000 recorded species of fish surrounding the islands, guests enjoy snorkeling, scuba diving, parasailing, boating and deep sea fishing.

Climate

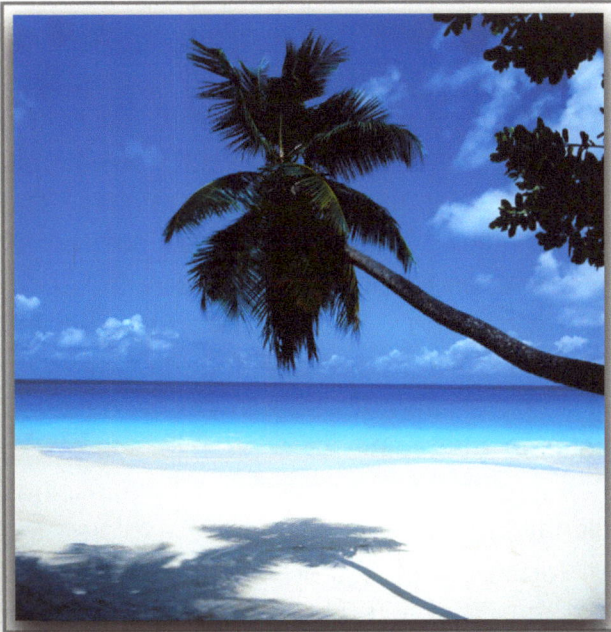

Seychelles lies outside the cyclone belt and is not prone to suffering tropical cyclones, hurricanes or tornadoes. Monsoon rains brought by the Northwest trade winds are common during the winter months from December to February. Annual rainfall averages from 288 centimeters in the capital city of Victoria to 355 centimeters on the hillside slopes. The sub-equatorial temperatures maintain an average of 26° to 28° Celsius and rarely falls below 23°C or exceeds 30°C. During the spring months of April and May and the autumn months of October and November, the tropical climate enables ocean water temperatures to reach 29°C with visibility as far as 30 meters or more.

Culture

As the islands of Seychelles had no original indigenous population, the current Seychellois are composed of emigrants. The largest ethnic groups are African, French, English, Indian and Chinese. Families tend to be led by dominant mothers and grandmothers who, in addition to leading active roles in society, take primary responsibility in raising their children and controlling household expenditures. The domestic role of men is more peripheral as they support their children and extended family financially. Since 1981 there has been a free educational system available to all children beginning at the age of 5 and requires attendance in grades 1 thru 9. Although well over 90% of Seychellois are educated according to English standards and receive an International General Certificate of Education (IGCSE), the culture remains emphatically French with approximately 70% of the population having a family name of French origin and 20% of English origin.

Economy

The main natural resources of Seychelles are fish, copra, cinnamon, coconut, salt and iron. Tourism, agriculture, fisheries, manufacturing and construction are all economic pillars of Seychelles, with the export of canned tuna and fresh fish bearing 83% of national exports (10% of total foreign exchange earnings). The Seychelles International Trade Zone (SITZ) consists of a series of companies involved in light manufacturing, processing, assembling, distribution, management operations and technology oriented businesses. Currently 60% of the country's population is employed by the private sector. SITZ assists the private sector in managing its economic and social development. The business community in Seychelles is extremely environmentally conscious and maintains a prosperous economy. Although multinational oil companies have explored the waters around the islands, no oil or gas has been found. Since there are no oil refining capabilities on the islands, oil and gas are imported at the rate of 5,700 barrels per day from the Gulf, Kuwait and Bahrain. Seychelles imports three times more oil than is needed for internal uses because it re-exports the surplus to ships and aircraft on Mahe island. Oil and gas imports, distribution and re-export are the responsibility of Seychelles Petroleum (Sepec) and oil exploration is the duty of Seychelles National Oil Company (SNOC). The Ministry of Information Technology and Communication is responsible for regulating the telecommunications sector. International fixed line and mobile communications are provided by Cable and Wireless and AirTel, while Atlas and Kokonet furnish high speed internet. Strict regulations and competition between companies ensures quality communications while tranquil weather patterns further assist in providing uninterrupted services. Air Seychelles, British Airways and Air France offer flights to major European destinations such as London, Paris, Rome, Munich and Zurich. There are more than one hundred flights to and from the Seychelles International Airport each week servicing over 150,000 tourists annually.

Geography

Under Schedule 1 (Part 1) of the Republic of Seychelles Constitution Seychelles consists of exactly 155 granite and coral islands and covers an economic zone of 1.4 million square kilometers in the Southwestern Indian Ocean. This pristine archipelago is located between 4 to 10 degrees south of the equator, northeast of Madagascar about 1,500 kilometers off the East coast of Africa. The largest island in the Republic of Seychelles is Mahe and at 148 square kilometers it constitutes one-third of the nation's total land area. Other notably sized islands are Silhouette, Praslin and La Digue, which are 20, 34 and 48 kilometers away from Mahe respectively.

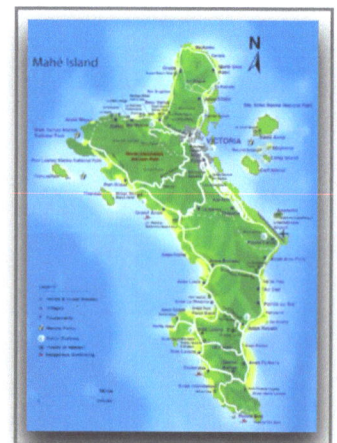

History

Arab traders were the first to have spotted the islands. During the 16th century French settlers arrived and later officially took possession of Seychelles in 1742. They started permanent settlements in 1770 and ruled Seychelles for 40 years. The islands later changed hands seven times between the French and the British. And in 1814 the Treaty of Paris incorporated both Seychelles and Mauritius as part of the British Empire. In 1903 Seychelles formally attained the status of a separate British Crown Colony. It wasn't until 1976 that Seychelles attained Independence. In 1992 Seychelles became a multi-party democracy and through a national referendum created a new Constitution in June of 1993. Seychelles is currently divided into twenty-five political districts, each with a seat on the National Assembly. The Seychelles People's Progressive Front (SPPF) recently surpassed the Seychelles Democratic Party (SDP) to win the presidency and a majority of seats in the National Assembly. The Seychelles legal system is based on English Common Law, Napoleonic Code and the Seychelles Constitution, while Civil Law is based on adapted Napoleonic Code. Seychelles Company Law is based on English Common Law. The highest court in the Judiciary is the Court of Appeal. The Republic of Seychelles is a member of the United Nations, African Union, Indian Ocean Commission and British Commonwealth. Seychelles has embassies in Paris and New York as well as numerous honorary consultants worldwide.

Interesting Facts

Capital
Victoria

Official Language
English, French
Seychellois Creole

Government
Republic

Laws
Common Law

Independence Day
June 29th, 1976

Total Area
450 Km2

Population
84,000

GDP
$767 Million

Currency
Seychelles Rupee (SCR)

Driving
Left

Internet
.sc

Calling Code
+248

Seychelles
Company Special License (CSL)

Introduction

A Seychelles Company Special License (CSL) pays only 1.5% tax on worldwide income and is designed to engage in all forms of international business. A CSL is of particular benefit for people who live in high-tax countries with intrusive regulatory environments and require the ability to demonstrate proper operation of a tax-paying or "tax resident" business with a local presence in the country of registration. A Company Special License is suited for investment management and advice, offshore banking, insurance and re-insurance, investments, holdings, intellectual property holdings, marketing, headquarters, human resources, franchises, business under a Seychelles International Trade Zone (SITZ) license or any other business approved by the Seychelles International Business Authority (SIBA).

Confidentiality and Privacy

The Republic of Seychelles is an independent nation and has avoided entering any information sharing agreements with other countries in exchange for foreign aid. Seychelles is also not subject to the EU Savings Tax Directive as are some United Kingdom overseas territories. Unless a person is wanted for serious international crimes and is being investigated by the Financial Intelligence Unit for something like money laundering or INTERPOL suspects them for human trafficking, the Republic of Seychelles does not share or report any information to overseas "principles" or organizations.

Republic of Seychelles — Company Special License (CSL)

Company Laws	Companies Ordinance, 1972
	Companies Special Licenses Act, 2003
Official Document Language	English
Conduct Business Internationally	Yes
Conduct Business in Seychelles	No
Resident Agent Required	Yes
Registered Office Required	Yes
Resident Secretary Required	Yes
Company Taxation	1.5 % of Worldwide Income
Double Taxation Avoidance Agreements	Yes
Company Tax Resident Qualification	Yes
Income Tax and Business Tax	Yes
Detailed Client Application Required	Yes *(Confidential)*
Seychelles International Business Authority	SIBA Application
Seychelles International Business Authority	SIBA Personal Questionnaire
Minimum Shareholders	2
Company Shareholders Allowed	Yes
Residency of Shareholders Allowed	Non-Seychellois
Register of Shareholders	In Private Possession of Registered Agent
Register of Shareholders Public Record	No
Bearer Shares Permitted	No
Minimum Directors	2
Company Directors Allowed	No
Residency of Directors Allowed	Any Nationality
Register of Directors	Yes
Register of Directors Public Record	Yes
Disclosure of Beneficial Owners to Reg. Agent	Yes *(Due Diligence Requirements)*
Disclosure of Beneficial Owners with Registrar	Yes *(Not Public)*
Annual General Meeting Required	Yes
Shareholders / Directors Meeting Required	Yes *(Anywhere in the World or by Proxy)*
Company Minutes and Resolutions	In Private Possession of Registered Agent
Company Seal Required	No
Minimum Paid Up Capital Required	10 % of the Authorized Capital
Maximum Authorized Capital Investment	Unlimited
Capital Considerations	Any Currency or in Kind / Seychelles Rupee
Subject to Currency Controls and Restrictions	No
Application Fees	$200
Annual Government Fees	$1,000
Keeping of Accounts Required	Yes
Filing of Accounts and Returns Required	Yes *(Not Public)*
Annual Government Return Filing Fees	$200
Auditing of Accounts Required	Yes
Re-Domicile From or To a Foreign Country	Yes
Shelf Companies Available	No
Incorporation Time	Within 1 Month

Paid Up Capital

A Seychelles CSL is required to have a minimum paid-up capital of 10% of the authorized capital in order to initiate business operations.

Business Plan

CSL applications must contain a business plan, provided by the beneficial owners, indicating company objectives, company operations, a 3-year financial forecast, market descriptions, marketing penetration strategies and details about the company capitalization.

Financial Reporting

A Seychelles Company Special License is required to prepare and file an annual financial accounts and returns to the Seychelles International Business Authority (SIBA). A Seychelles CSL is free to arrange its business accounts in any manner fitting to establish and maintain reasonable accuracy of the company's financial position.

Government Licensing Fees

Seychelles Companies Special Licenses Act, 2003
Schedule 3 - Fees (Section 23)

(a) An application for incorporation $200 (USD)
(b) Annual license fee $1,000 (USD)
(c) Annual return filing fee $200 (USD)

Names

Seychelles Companies Special Licenses Act, 2003
Schedule 19 - Reservation of Name

The Authority may reserve the proposed name of a relevant company pending the incorporation of that company and issue a certificate stating the name so reserved if an application is made for that purpose in the prescribed manner.

Name Endings

CSL	Company Special License

Secretarial Requirements

Seychelles Companies Special Licenses Act, 2003
Schedule 13 - Secretary

(1) *A relevant company shall at all times have a secretary of the company and such secretary shall be a resident of Seychelles or a body corporate incorporated in Seychelles.*

(2) *All applications made and all documents required to be submitted to the Registrar or the Authority under any Act by a relevant company shall be made or submitted through the secretary who or which shall verify in writing the signature of any person appearing on the application or document.*

(3) *The secretary may accept service on behalf of the relevant company and any service accepted by the secretary shall be deemed to have been accepted by the company.*

Shares

A Seychelles CSL may only issue registered shares. Company shares may be designated as:

1.) No Par Value   **3.)** Preferred   **5.)** Voting
2.) Non-Voting   **4.)** Redeemable

Bearer Shares

Bearer shares are prohibited.

Taxation

Seychelles Companies Special Licenses Act, 2003
Schedule 2 - Rates of Tax (Section 21)

1. *The rate of the tax payable by a relevant company in respect of its taxable income is 1.5%.*
2. *The rates of withholding tax under Part IV of the Business Tax Act are as follows–*
    (a) *in respect of dividend paid to a resident - Nil*
    (b) *in respect of dividend paid to a non-resident - Nil*
    (c) *in respect of interest paid to a resident - Nil*
    (d) *in respect of interest paid to a non-resident - Nil*
    (e) *in respect of royalty paid to a non-resident for the use of, or the right to use, any copyright. patent, design or model or plan or trademark - Nil*
    (f) *in respect of royalty paid to a non-resident in respect of the supply of scientific, technical, industrial or commercial knowledge, information or services - Nil*
    (g) *in respect of royalty paid to a non-resident for the use of, or the right to use, any secret formula, process or know-how whether the know-how is technical, managerial or otherwise and any other intellectual property or right - Nil*
    (h) *in respect of royalty paid to a non-resident for the use of, or the right to use, any industrial, commercial or scientific equipment - Nil*

Double Taxation Avoidance Agreement (DTAA)

The Republic of Seychelles has signed and ratified double taxation avoidance agreements in 13 countries with 3 countries pending ratification and 7 countries under negotiation.

DTAA Signed and Ratified	DTAA Pending Ratification	DTAA Under Negotiation
Barbados	Belgium	Bahrain
Botswana	Monaco	Czech Republic
China	Zimbabwe	Egypt
Cyprus		Kuwait
Indonesia		Namibia
Malaysia		Russia
Mauritius		Tunisia
Oman		
Qatar		
South Africa		
Thailand		
United Arab Emirates		
Vietnam		

Seychelles
Foundation

Introduction

Over 60% of the world is under a civil law form of government including most of Europe and all of Asia, with the exception of Hong Kong and Singapore. Foundations are widely excepted in the international community and preferred in most countries operating under civil law. A Seychelles Foundation is a separate legal entity just like a company, but has beneficiaries rather than shareholders. Assets transferred to a foundation become the property of the foundation with full legal and beneficial title and are no longer the assets of the founder. Once a foundation has been funded it is managed by a foundation council for the directing of investments and appointment and removal of councillors, protectors and beneficiaries. The foundation council is located in the Republic of Seychelles, which is a nil tax jurisdiction, and mitigates potential tax risks from aggressive taxing authorities in other countries.

Republic of Seychelles — Foundation

Foundation Laws	Foundations Act, 2003
Official Document Language	English
Conduct Business Internationally	Yes
Conduct Business in Republic of Seychelles	Yes
Resident Agent Required	Yes *(Foundation Service Provider)*
Registered Office Required	Yes *(Foundation Service Provider)*
Resident Secretary Required	No
Company Taxation	0 % of Worldwide Income
Double Taxation Avoidance Agreements	No
Company Tax Resident Qualification	No
Income Tax and Business Tax	No
Detailed Client Application Required	No
Minimum Founders	1
Company Founders Allowed	Yes
Residency of Founders Allowed	Non-Seychellois
Register of Founders	In Private Possession of Registered Agent
Register of Founders Public Record	Yes *(Nominee Founders Permitted)*
Minimum Councillors	1
Company Councillors Allowed	Yes
Residency of Councillors Allowed	Any Nationality
Register of Councillors	In Private Possession of Registered Agent
Register of Councillors Public Record	No
Disclosure of Beneficiaries to Reg. Agent	Yes *(Due Diligence Requirements)*
Disclosure of Beneficiaries with Registrar	No
Annual General Meeting Required	Yes *(Anywhere in the World or by Proxy)*
Foundation Minutes and Resolutions	In Private Possession of Registered Agent
Minimum Funding	$1
Capital Considerations	Any Currency or in Kind
Subject to Currency Controls and Restrictions	No
Application Fees	No
Annual Government Fees	$230 First Year *($215 Thereafter)*
Keeping of Accounts Required	Yes
Filing of Accounts and Returns Required	No
Annual Government Return Filing Fees	No
Auditing of Accounts Required	No
Re-Domicile from a Foreign Country	Yes
Re-Domicile to a Foreign Country	Yes
Shelf Foundations Available	Yes
Incorporation Time	1 Business Day

Books and Records
Foundations Act, 2009

(1) *A Foundation shall keep proper books of account and records as its council considers necessary in order to reflect its financial position, about —*

(a) *all sums of money received, expended and distributed by the Foundation, and the matters about which the receipt, expenditure and distribution took place;*

(b) *all sales and purchases by the Foundation; and*

(c) *the assets and liabilities of the Foundation.*

Foundation
Founder

The founder is the person who is creating the foundation and may be any individual, legal entity or nominee. Seychelles foundations permit two or more co-founders. A founder, or another person assigned the rights of the founder in the Charter or Regulations, may reserve special rights to direct investments, appoint and remove beneficiaries, or even dissolve the foundation. A founder may even be the sole beneficiary of the foundation during his lifetime, so long as successors are appointed.

Councillor

The councillor manages the business affairs of the foundation and may be natural individuals or legal entities. A minimum of one councillor is required. Councillors may be of any nationality and reside anywhere in the world. A founder may be councillor, but not the sole councillor.

Protector

A protector is the person who oversees the trustee and activities of the trust. The foundation may appoint a protector if provisioned in the Charter or Regulations. A sole councillor or sole beneficiary may not act as a protector.

Beneficiary

Beneficiaries receive the distribution of assets according the Charter or Regulations. However, beneficiaries of a Seychelles foundation are not owners and have no rights or control over the assets belonging to the foundation.

Funding

A Seychelles Foundation must have initial assets of $1 minimum. Assets may originate from any lawful source either from the founder or a third party and may consist of present or future assets of any nature. In addition to non-Seychelles assets, the foundation may include the following Seychelles assets:

Foundations Act, 2009
Part II - Establishment of Foundations
Section 11 - Assets of Foundation

(1) The assets of a Foundation —
   (a) may include —
   (i) any interest or entitlement as a beneficiary of another Foundation registered under this Act;
   (ii) any shares, debentures or other interests in a company incorporated under the International Business Companies Act;
   (iii) any shares, debentures or other interests in a company licensed under the Companies (Special Licenses) Act;
   (iv) any shares, debentures or other interests in a company incorporated under the Protected Cell Companies Act;
   (v) any interest in a partnership registered under the Limited Partnerships Act;
   (vi) any interest or entitlement as a beneficiary under a trust registered under the International Trusts Act;
   (vii) any company, trust or other entity licensed as a mutual fund under the Mutual Fund and Hedge Fund Act; or
   (viii) any funds in an account with a bank licensed under the Financial Institutions Act; and
   (b) shall not include immovable properties or other properties in Seychelles, including shares, debentures or other interests in a legal person incorporated or registered, in Seychelles.

(2) to the written laws, lease immovable properties in Seychelles, only for any of the purposes mentioned in section 7(2)(c)(v).

Government Licensing Fees

Annual government licensing fees are $200 per year (plus tax of $30 in year one and $15 thereafter) due annually upon the original registration date.

Names

The name may be in any language, but if the name is other than English or French it must be accompanied with one of the two respective language translations.

Name Endings

Foundation

Regulations

A foundation may adopt a document entitled Regulations, which is private and not filed with the registry. The Regulations may, for example, provide for the identification and designation of councillors, beneficiaries, distribution of the foundation assets and beneficiary entitlement proportions.

Rules of Operation

A Seychelles Foundation is created for the management and distribution of assets in accordance with the Charter or Regulations for the purpose of either family succession as a "private foundation", for charitable causes as a "charity foundation", for a specified reason as a "purpose foundation" or any combinations of the three.

Taxation

Income and distributions to beneficiaries are completely exempt from taxation in Seychelles even if "managed and controlled" by a Foundation Council from Seychelles.

Seychelles
International Business Company (IBC)

Introduction

A Seychelles International Business Company (IBC) is a tax-free company designed to engage in all forms of international business with strict owner privacy laws, minimal record keeping and no reporting requirements. Since the introduction of the Seychelles International Business Companies Act in 1994, more than 600 new companies are formed every month, totaling over 30,000 registered Seychelles IBC's. An International Business Company is suited for management consultants, network engineers, software developers, professionals who tend to travel between various countries on short-term assignments, internet based businesses, international commodity trading or any other business approved by the Seychelles International Business Authority. A Seychelles IBC may be used as a personal asset protection vehicle to passively hold property and investments.

Republic of Seychelles — International Business Company (IBC)

Company Laws	International Business Companies Act, 1994
Official Document Language	English
Conduct Business Internationally	Yes
Conduct Business in Seychelles	No
Resident Agent / Registered Office Required	Yes
Resident Secretary Required	No
Company Taxation	0 % of Worldwide Income
Double Taxation Avoidance Agreements	No
Company Tax Resident Qualification	No
Income Tax and Business Tax	No
Detailed Client Application Required	No
Minimum Shareholders	1
Company Shareholders Allowed	Yes
Residency of Shareholders Allowed	Non-Seychellois
Register of Shareholders	In Private Possession of Registered Agent
Register of Shareholders Public Record	No
Bearer Shares Permitted	No
Minimum Directors	1
Company Directors Allowed	Yes
Residency of Directors Allowed	Any Nationality
Register of Directors	In Private Possession of Registered Agent
Register of Directors Public Record	No
Disclosure of Beneficial Owners to Reg. Agent	Yes *(Due Diligence Requirements)*
Disclosure of Beneficial Owners with Registrar	No
Annual General Meeting Required	No
Shareholders / Directors Meeting Required	Yes *(Anywhere in the World or by Proxy)*
Company Minutes and Resolutions	In Private Possession of Registered Agent
Company Seal Required	No
Minimum Paid Up Capital Required	No
Maximum Authorized Capital Investment	Unlimited
Capital Considerations	Any Currency or in Kind
Subject to Currency Controls and Restrictions	No
Application Fees	No
Annual Government Fees	$100
Keeping of Accounts Required	Yes
Filing of Accounts and Returns Required	No
Annual Government Return Filing Fees	No
Auditing of Accounts Required	No
Re-Domicile From and To a Foreign Country	Yes
Shelf Companies Available	Yes
Incorporation Time	1 Business Day

Name Endings

AG	Aktiengesellschaft
AO	Aktsionernoye Obschestvo
ApS	Anpartsselskab
AS	Akciová Společnost or Akciová Spoločnosť
A/S	Aktieselskab
Bhd	Berhad
BV	Besloten Vennootschap
CC	Close Corporation
CIE	Compagnie
CO	Company
Corp	Corporation
DD	Delniska Druzba or Dioníčko Društvo
EPE	Eteria Periorismenis Efthynis
Est	Anstalt
GmbH	Gesellschaft mit beschränkter Haftung
Inc	Incorporated
LLC	Limited Life Company
Ltd	Limited
LTDA	Limita
NV	Namloze Vennootschap
oo	Private Limited Company
OY	Osakkeyhtiä or Osakeyhtiö
PLC	Public Limited Company
Pty	Proprietary
(Pty) Ltd	(Proprietory) Limited
RT	Részvény Társaság or Részvénytársaság
SA	Société Anonyme or Sociedad Anomina
SARL	Societe A Responosabilité Limité
SL	Sociedad Limitada
SPA	Società Per Azioni
Spz	Spólka z organiczoną odpowiedzialnoścoą
Srl	Società a responsabilità limitada
SRO	Spolecnost s. Rvcenin Omezenym

Government Licensing Fees

Regardless of the amount of authorized capital, paid up capital or total number of shares in a Seychelles IBC, the annual government licensing fee is $100 (USD). Should the assets of an IBC be valued in the millions or even tens of millions of dollars, this annual licensing fee remains the same. In comparison to other tax havens, this flat annual licensing fee with an unlimited amount of authorized capital is arguably one of the most competitive in the world.

Name Restrictions

Seychelles International Business Companies Act, 1994
Part II - Constitution of Companies (Section 11)

(3) *No company shall be incorporated under this Act under a name that -*
   (a)   *is identical with that of a statutory corporation or that under which a company in existence is already incorporated under this Act or registered under the Companies Act or so nearly resembles the name of another company as to be calculated to deceive, except where the company in existence gives its consent;*
   (b)   *contains the words "Assurance", "Bank", "Building Society", "Chamber of Commerce", "Chartered, "Cooperative", "Imperial". "Insurance", "Municipal", "Trust", "Foundation", or a word conveying a similar meaning, or any other word that, in the opinion of the Registrar, suggests or is calculated to suggest the patronage of or any connection with Seychelles or the Government of Seychelles or with any other country or the Government of that country:Provided however that the Registrar may permit the incorporation of a company under a name that includes the word "Seychelles" if the Registrar thinks fit to do so;",*
   (c)   *is indecent, offensive or, in the opinion of the Registrar is otherwise objectionable or misleading.*

Rules of Operation

Seychelles International Business Companies Act, 1994
Part II - Constitution of Companies (Section 5 / *Edited*)

(1) *For the purposes of this Act, an International Business Company is a company that does not –*
   (a) carry on business in Seychelles;
   (b) own an interest in (or lease) immovable property situate in Seychelles . . .;
   (c) carry on banking . . . or a trust business;
   (d) carry on business as an insurance or a reinsurance company; or
   (e) carry on the business of providing the registered office for companies.

(2) . . . *an International Business Company shall not be treated as carrying on business in Seychelles by reason only that -*

(a)   it makes or maintains deposits with a person carrying on business within Seychelles;

(b)   it makes or maintains professional contact with counsel and attorneys, accountants, bookkeepers, trust companies, management companies, investment advisers or other similar persons carrying on business within Seychelles;

(c)   it prepares or maintains books and records within Seychelles;

(d)   it holds, within Seychelles, meetings of its directors or members;

(e)   it holds a lease of property for use as an office from which to communicate with members or where books and records of the company are prepared or maintained;

(f)   it holds shares, debt obligations or other securities in a (Seychelles IBC);

(g)   it holds bonds, treasury bills and other securities issued by the Government of Seychelles or the Central Bank of Seychelles;

(h)   shares, debt obligations or other securities in the company are owned by any person resident in Seychelles . . . ; or

(i)   it owns or manages a (shipping) vessel (or an aircraft) registered in (the Republic of Seychelles).

Shares

A Seychelles IBC may issue registered shares or bearer shares. Company shares may be designated as:

1.) Common

2.) No Par Value

3.) Non-Voting

4.) Preferred

5.) Redeemable

6.) Unnumbered

7.) Voting

8.) Shares having more or less than one vote per share

9.) Shares that may be voted only when held by persons who meet specified requirements

10.) Shares that entitle participation only on certain assets

11.) Shares that may be voted only on certain matters

12.) Shares that may be voted only upon the occurrence of certain events

Bearer Shares

The legal restrictions on bearer shares largely negates any benefits as the issuance and transfer of bearer shares cannot be carried out anonymously. A further hindrance to the use of bearer shares are the reluctance of banks to open accounts for bearer share companies.

Seychelles International Business Companies Act, 1994
Part III - Capital and Dividends
Section 28

(1   A company incorporated under this Act shall cause to be kept one or more registers to be known as Share Registers containing -

(a)   the names and addresses of the persons who hold registered shares in the company;

(b)   the number of each class and series of registered shares held by each person;

(c)   the date on which the name of each person was entered in the Share Register;

(d)   the date on which any person ceased to be a member;

(e)   in the case of shares issued to bearer, the total number of each class and series of shares issued to bearer;

(f)   with respect to each certificate for shares issued to bearer -

(i)   the identifying number of the certificate;

(ii)   the number of each class or series of shares issued to bearer specified therein, and

(iii)   the date of issue of the certificate; but the company may delete from the Share Register information relating to shares issued to bearer that have been cancelled.

Taxation

By legal definition, a Seychelles IBC and its shareholders are not subject to any tax or duty derived from income or profits, stamp duties on all transfers of property, transactions of shares, debt obligations and other securities.

Seychelles International Business Companies Act, 1994
Part XI - Exemptions (Section 109)

(1)   A company incorporated under this Act or a shareholder thereof shall not be subject to any tax or duty on income or profits accruing to or deriving from such company or in connection with any transaction to which that company or shareholder, as the case may be, is a party.

(2)   Notwithstanding any provision of the Stamp Duty Act 1975 -

(a)   all transfers of property to or by a company incorporated under this Act;

(b)   all transactions in respect of the shares, debt obligations or other securities of a company incorporated under this Act; and

(c)   all other transactions relating to the business of a company incorporated under this Act, are exempt from the payment of stamp duty.

Seychelles
International Trust

Introduction

A Seychelles International Trust is an irrevocable trust established generally in perpetuity of 100 years. Often a Private Trust Company (PTC) may be created using an international trust as a revocable instrument in order to retain varying levels of control of the trust without jeopardizing the 'validity' of the trust. The Seychelles Court has jurisdiction for all matters relating to a Seychelles International Trust and any transfers of property into the trust may not be voided or invalidated due to any foreign rule of forced heirship. A Seychelles International Trust will also remain in full effect even if the trust concept is not recognized or admitted under the laws of a foreign jurisdiction.

Republic of Seychelles   International Trust

Trust Laws	International Trust Act, 1994
Official Document Language	English
Resident Agent Required	Yes
Registered Office Required	Yes
Resident Secretary Required	No
Trust Taxation	0 % of Worldwide Income
Double Taxation Avoidance Agreements	No
Income Tax and Business Tax	No
Detailed Client Application Required	No
Minimum Settlors	1
Company Settlors Allowed	Yes
Residency of Settlors Allowed	Non-Seychellois
Register of Settlors	In Private Possession of Registered Agent
Register of Settlors Public Record	No
Minimum Trustees	1
Company Trustees Allowed	Yes
Residency of Trustees Allowed	Yes *(International Trust Service Provider)*
Register of Trustees	In Private Possession of Registered Agent
Register of Trustees Public Record	No
Company Protectors Allowed	Yes
Disclosure of Beneficiaries to Reg. Agent	Yes *(Due Diligence Requirements)*
Disclosure of Beneficiaries with Registrar	No
Annual General Meeting Required	No
Minimum Funding	$1
Capital Considerations	Any Currency or in Kind
Subject to Currency Controls and Restrictions	No
Application Fees	$100
Annual Government Fees	No
Keeping of Accounts Required	Yes
Filing of Accounts and Returns Required	No
Annual Government Return Filing Fees	No
Auditing of Accounts Required	No
Re-Domicile from a Foreign Country	Yes
Re-Domicile to a Foreign Country	Yes
Shelf Trusts Available	No
Registration Time	1 Business Day

Books and Records

A Seychelles International Trust is required to maintain accounting records.

Funding

A Seychelles International Trust may include anything not specifically mentioned in the International Trust Act.

International Trust Act, 1994
Part VIII - Protective Trusts, Class Interests and Exercise of Certain Power
Section 56 - Permitted investments

(1) *Subject to Section 4, the terms of an international trust may authorize the trustees to invest trust property in securities and investments with or without conditions or restriction.*

International Trust Act, 1994
Part II - General Provisions (Section 4 - International Trust)

(1) *An international trust is a trust or a constructive trust in respect of which -*
   (c) *the trust property does not . . . include -*
      (i) *any property situated in Seychelles.*

Government Licensing Fees

Although there is an initial $100 government fee, there are no annual government fees for a Seychelles International Trust.

Names

The Trust Deed is a private document and not filed publicly and may therefore be named in any manner desired. Generally, the type of trust is listed in the trust name.

Name Endings

Trust
International Trust
Charitable Trust
Purpose Trust

Rules of Operation

A Seychelles International Trust is created for the management and distribution of assets in accordance with the trust agreement for the purpose of estate planning and family succession, charitable causes as in a charitable trust or other specified reasons as in a purpose trust.

Taxation

A Seychelles International Trust is completely exempt from business tax, withholding tax, capital gains tax and stamp duty in Seychelles.

Trust

Settlor

A settlor is the person who created the trust. A settlor of a Seychelles International Trust may be an individual or a legal entity. A settlor may not be a resident of Seychelles at any time during the existence of the trust.

Trustee

A trustee is the person who holds and disburses the assets of the trust. A Seychelles International Trust permits a trustee to be an individual or legal entity residing absolutely anywhere in the world. At all times there must be at least one Seychelles resident trustee who is a licensed International Trustee Service Provider. A settlor may be a trustee, but not the sole trustee.

Protector

A protector, sometimes known as a compliance enforcer, is the person who oversees the trustee and activities of the trust. The appointment of a protector must be provided for in the Trust. A protector is generally given powers for the appointment and removal of trustees. The rights for a Protector to amend the Trust Deed must be clearly indicated in the Deed.

Beneficiary
International Trust Act, 1994
Part III - Creation of International Trusts
Section 17 - Beneficiaries of an International Trust

(1) *A beneficiary shall be -*
   (a) identifiable by name; or
   (b) ascertainable by reference to -
      (i)   a class; or
      (ii)   a relationship to another person, whether or not living at the time of the creation of the trust or at the time by reference to which, under the terms of the trust, members of a class are to be determined.

Seychelles
Limited Partnership (LP)

Introduction

A Seychelles Limited Partnership (LP) is used in large part for international joint ventures and fund management. Since a Limited Partnership is a flow-throw tax entity, a Seychelles LP may receive income from sources outside Seychelles and be distributed to various international partners without incurring a Seychelles tax liability. This strategy allows for each partner to be responsible for their respective tax liabilities in their resident country without sustaining any additional tax consequences for their joint venture operation or investment funds in Seychelles. Although a Seychelles LP is prohibited from conducting any business activities within the Republic of Seychelles, the Limited Partnership is still required to have a Seychelles resident agent and registered office for the service of process and delivery of legal notice.

Republic of Seychelles   Limited Partnership

Partnership Laws	Limited Partnerships Act, 2003
Official Document Language	English
Conduct Business Internationally	Yes
Conduct Business in Seychelles	No
Resident Agent Required	No
Registered Office Required	No
Resident Secretary Required	No
Company Taxation	Fiscally Transparent *(Flow-thru to Partners)*
Double Taxation Avoidance Agreements	No
Company Tax Resident Qualification	Yes
Income Tax and Business Tax	Yes
Detailed Client Application Required	No
Minimum Partners	2
Minimum General Partners	1 *(Must be a Seychelles Resident or Entity)*
Minimum Limited Partners	1
Corporate Partners Allowed	Yes
Residency of Partners Allowed	Any Nationality
Register of Partners	Yes
Register of Partners Public Record	Yes *(Only General Partners on Public Record)*
Disclosure of Beneficial Owners to Reg. Agent	Yes *(Due Diligence Requirements)*
Disclosure of Beneficial Owners with Registrar	No *(Not if Partners are Offshore Entities)*
Annual General Meeting Required	No
Partners Meeting Required	Yes *(Anywhere in the World or by Proxy)*
Partnership Minutes and Resolutions	Yes
Partnership Seal Required	No
Minimum Paid Up Capital Required	$2
Maximum Authorized Capital Investment	*(Not Applicable)*
Capital Considerations	Any Currency or in Kind
Subject to Currency Controls and Restrictions	No
Application Fees	No
Annual Government Fees	$200
Keeping of Accounts Required	Yes
Filing of Accounts and Returns Required	Yes
Annual Government Return Filing Fees	Yes
Auditing of Accounts Required	Yes
Re-Domicile from a Foreign Country	Yes
Re-Domicile to a Foreign Country	Yes
Shelf Partnerships Available	No
Incorporation Time	1 Business Day

Paid Up Capital

The minimum Paid Up Capital for a Seychelles Limited Partnership is $2.

Confidentiality and Privacy

At least one of the general partners in a Seychelles Limited Partnership must a Seychelles entity, such as a Seychelles International Business Company (IBC). A Statement of Particulars is required to be filled with the Registry disclosing the names and addresses of the general partner(s). However this registration process does not disclose any information on the limited partners, nor is the partnership agreement filed at the Registry.

Financial Reporting

A Seychelles Limited Partnership is required to prepare and file annual financial accounts and may be subject to audits. The partnership is free to arrange its business accounts in any manner fitting to establish and maintain reasonable accuracy of the partnership's financial position.

Government Licensing Fees

The annual licensing fees for a Seychelles Limited Partnership is $200.

Name Endings

LP	Limited Partnership

Partnership

General Partner

The General Partner acts in many regards like the general in an army and is responsible for the administration and management of the LP by signing letters, contracts, deeds and documents and making official decisions on behalf of the Limited Partnership. The General Partner has 100% unlimited liability for any debts and obligations that exceed the assets of the Limited Partnership. A General Partner may also be a Limited Partner.

(4)(2) *A limited partnership shall consist of one or more persons called general partners who shall, in the event that the assets of the limited partnership are inadequate, be liable for all the debts and obligations of the limited partnership and one or more persons called limited partners who shall not be liable for the debts or obligations of the limited partnership . . .*

Limited Partner

Limited Partners are just that; they are limited. A Limited Partner may invest financial resources into the LP, but is not authorized to participate in the administration and management aspects the Limited Partnership. Due to their passive role, Limited Partners are protected from any debts and obligations of the LP provided they do not conduct themselves in a manner befitting a General Partner. Otherwise, a Limited Partner is liable for claims against the partnership only up to the amount of their contribution to the Limited Partnership.

Partnership Interests

Partnership interests are equal, unless otherwise prescribed in writing by agreement between the partners.

Rules of Operation

Limited Partnerships Act, 2003
Part II - General (Section 4(1) - Constitution)

(4)(1) *A limited partnership may be formed under this Act for any lawful purpose: Provided that a limited partnership shall not carry on business in Seychelles except so far as may be necessary for the carrying on of the business of that limited partnership outside Seychelles.*

Taxation

A Seychelles Limited Partnership is a flow-through tax entity and is not liable for any Seychelles taxation on profits or gains arising from within the partnership. The respective partners are liable to file their own respective tax returns and may have tax liabilities in their resident country.

Seychelles
Protected Cell Company (PCC)

Introduction

A Seychelles Protected Cell Company (PCC) is an entity designed specifically for the use of insurance companies, mutual funds and hedge funds. A PCC consists of a "core" and unlimited number of segregated "cells". Each cell is deemed an isolated unit capable of engaging in contractual obligations unique to the assets within the cell without involving assets from any other cells or jeopardizing them to the reach of creditors. This separation of assets provided by the cells protects insurance companies in the event of catastrophe and minimizes loss for companies heavily vested in securitization instruments subject to risk. There are very few Protected Cell Companies in existence in Seychelles and until authorities permit additional uses for this structure, applications will only be considered if the business involves captive insurance or umbrella funds.

Republic of Seychelles — Protected Cell Company

Company Laws	Companies Ordinance, 1972
	Protected Cell Companies Act, 2003
Official Document Language	English
Conduct Business Internationally	Yes
Conduct Business in Seychelles	Yes
Resident Agent / Registered Office Required	Yes
Resident Secretary Required	Yes
Company Taxation	1.5 % of Worldwide Income
Double Taxation Avoidance Agreements	Yes
Company Tax Resident Qualification	Yes
Income Tax and Business Tax	Yes
Detailed Client Application Required	Yes *(Confidential)*
Seychelles International Business Authority	SIBA Application Guidelines
Seychelles International Business Authority	SIBA Application
Minimum Shareholders	2
Company Shareholders Allowed	No
Residency of Shareholders Allowed	Non-Seychellois
Register of Shareholders	In Private Possession of Registered Agent
Register of Shareholders Public Record	No
Bearer Shares Permitted	No
Minimum Directors	2
Company Directors Allowed	No
Residency of Directors Allowed	Any Nationality
Register of Directors	Public
Register of Directors Public Record	Yes
Disclosure of Beneficial Owners to Reg. Agent	Yes *(Due Diligence Requirements)*
Disclosure of Beneficial Owners with Registrar	No
Annual General Meeting Required	No
Shareholders / Directors Meeting Required	Yes *(Anywhere in the World or by Proxy)*
Company Minutes and Resolutions	In Private Possession of Registered Agent
Company Seal Required	No
Minimum Paid Up Capital Required	10 % of the Authorized Capital
Maximum Authorized Capital Investment	Unlimited
Capital Considerations	Any Currency or in Kind / Seychelles Rupee
Subject to Currency Controls and Restrictions	Yes
Application Fees	$200
Annual Government Fees	$1,000
Keeping of Accounts Required	Yes
Filing of Accounts and Returns Required	Yes *(Not Public)*
Annual Government Return Filing Fees	$200
Auditing of Accounts Required	Yes
Re-Domicile From a Foreign Country	Yes
Re-Domicile to a Foreign Country	No
Shelf Companies Available	No
Incorporation Time	Within 1 Month

Paid Up Capital

A Seychelles PCC is required to have a minimum paid-up capital of 10% of the authorized capital in order to initiate business operations.

Business Plan

PCC applications must contain a business plan, provided by the beneficial owners, indicating company objectives, company operations, a 3-year financial forecast, market descriptions, marketing penetration strategies and details about the company capitalization.

Financial Reporting

A Seychelles Protected Cell Company is required to prepare and file an annual financial accounts and returns to the Seychelles International Business Authority (SIBA). A Seychelles PCC is free to arrange its business accounts in any manner fitting to establish and maintain reasonable accuracy of the company's financial position.

Government Licensing Fees

(a) An application for incorporation $200 (USD)
(b) Annual license fee $1,000 (USD)
(c) Annual return filing fee $200 (USD)

Names

The Seychelles International Business Authority may reserve the proposed name of a relevant company pending the incorporation of that company and issue a certificate stating the name so reserved if an application is made for that purpose in the prescribed manner.

Name Endings

PCC	Protected Cell Company

Secretarial Requirements

A Seychelles PCC is required at all times to have a local Seychelles secretary of the company.

Shares

A Seychelles PCC may only issue registered shares. Company shares may be designated as:
1.) Cellular   **2.)** Non-Cellular

Bearer Shares

Bearer shares are prohibited.

Structuring

Seychelles Protected Cell Companies Act, 2003
Part II - Formations and Attributes (Section 3 - Protected Cell Companies)

(2) *For the avoidance of doubt, it is hereby declared that notwithstanding that a protected cell company may have created one or more cells pursuant to the provisions of this Act-*
(a)   a protected cell company is a single legal person, and
(b)   the creation by a protected cell company of a cell does not create, in respect of that cell, a legal person separate from the company.

Seychelles Protected Cell Companies Act, 2003
Part II - Formations and Attributes (Section 4 - Creation of Cells)

A protected cell company may create one or more cells for the purpose of segregating and protecting cellular assets in the manner provided by this Act.

Double Taxation Avoidance Agreement (DTAA)

The Republic of Seychelles has signed and ratified double taxation avoidance agreements in 13 countries with 3 countries pending ratification and 7 countries under negotiation.

DTAA Signed and Ratified	DTAA Pending Ratification	DTAA Under Negotiation
Barbados	Belgium	Bahrain
Botswana	Monaco	Czech Republic
China	Zimbabwe	Egypt
Cyprus		Kuwait
Indonesia		Namibia
Malaysia		Russia
Mauritius		Tunisia
Oman		
Qatar		
South Africa		
Thailand		
United Arab Emirates		
Vietnam		

St Kitts & Nevis

About St Kitts & Nevis

Activities

The twin-island nation of St. Kitts & Nevis offers a wide array of outdoor activities. Nevis invites visitors to the Botanical Gardens, an 11 mile hike up Nevis Peak, snorkeling at Oualie, and relaxing on 3-mile long Pinney's Beach. St. Kitts has a scenic railway, beautiful arts and crafts unique to the country, plantation home tours, and the famous Brimestone Hill Fortress. Together the islands provide deep sea fishing, world renowned golfing, hiking, hot springs, mountain biking, ocean kayaking, para-sailing, scuba diving, swimming, windsurfing, and more.

Climate

St. Kitts & Nevis enjoys a tropical marine climate with a typical wet and dry season. Northeasterly trade winds and regional oceanic cyclones can have a profound influence on the local weather patterns. Generally the islands have warm and consistent temperatures averaging 24°C to 27°C with a humidity rate of only 71%. Rainfall levels increase with altitude as annual precipitation ranges from 40 cm in the coastal areas to 152 cm in the central mountains. The moderate rainy season is considered to last from May to October, with the heaviest accumulations occurring during July and August.

Culture

The culture of St. Kitts & Nevis could best be described as festive and vibrant with a variety of carnivals and outdoor celebrations taking place throughout the year. Over 50% of the country is actively religious and the primary denomination is Catholic. Christmas in particular is an extremely social time of year with the Carnival Masquerade, the National Carnival Queen Pageant, the Miss Caribbean Talented Teen Pageant, and the Junior Calypso Show. In the summer the island of St. Kitts hosts a musical festival including jazz, salsa, soca, calypso, and steelpan music. In keeping with the "Pirates of the Caribbean" spirit, St. Kitts & Nevis is known for its rum manufacturing distilled from local sugar cane.

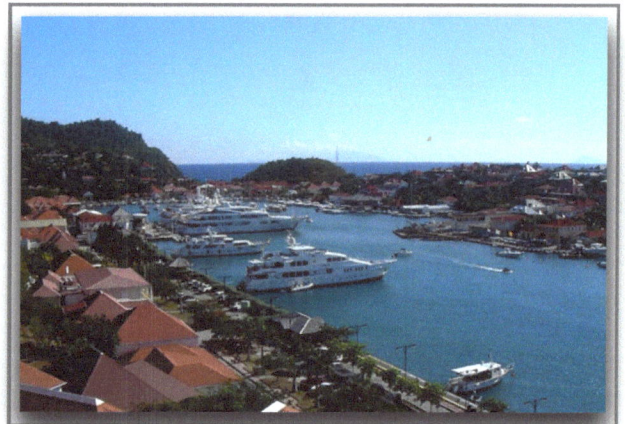

Economy and Offshore Financial Services

The economy of St. Kitts & Nevis traditionally lied within the sugar cane industry, however tourism, manufacturing, salt mining, and offshore banking have replaced a large percentage of the overall economy. Although 39% of the total land area is devoted to crops (the two primary crops are sugar cane and peanuts), the vast majority of produce and poultry is required to be imported along with key energy resources such as natural gas and oil. Local harvests of sweet potatoes, onions, tomatoes, cabbage, carrots, and fish help supply the community, but the demand for agricultural products and common staple goods require scheduled imports from the U.S and Canada. St. Kitts and Nevis is a member of the Eastern Caribbean Currency Union (ECCU), the Eastern Caribbean Central Bank (ECCB), and the Eastern Caribbean Telecommunications (ECTEL) Authority. Asset Protection Services of America offers the St. Kitts & Nevis citizenship by investment program as well as incorporation services for Business Companies, Citizenship by Investment, Foundations, International Exempt Trusts and Limited Liability Companies.

Geography

St. Kitts & Nevis is located in the Leeward Islands in the West Indies and has a total land mass of just 270 square kilometers. Saint Kitts is a longitudinal island at 180 square kilometers while the smaller island Nevis, which sits 3 kilometers to the south of St. Kitts, has a total land mass of 93 square kilometers. Both islands are comprised primarily of volcanic rock. The virtually round island of Nevis features the highest national point that is a dormant volcano called Mount Liamuiga at 1,156 meters above sea level. St. Kitts is home to a 270 acre great salt pond natural preserve for a wide range of biodiversity.

History

The islands of St. Kitts & Nevis were alleged to have been first spotted by Christopher columbus in 1493. In time the islands became known to ship captains for their fresh water, fertile soil, and large salt deposits. In 1624 the colony of Saint Christopher became the first English colony in the Caribbean. One year later the French joined the English colony in an attempt to out-populate the local Kalinago, whom had grown suspicious of the foreign presence. Such suspicion proved accurate as the combined English and French forces committed genocide murdering over 2,000 Kalinago men. Their bodies were dumped into a river where the blood was said to flow for days giving rise to the name "Bloody River". The few remaining Kalinago Indians were then deported. The islands remained a strategic military outpost for centuries and a central location of slave labor to harvest tobacco, sugar cane and salt. The French, English and Spanish fought over control of the islands until the Treaty of Ultrecht was signed in 1713, which ceded St. Kitts to the British in perpetuity.

Interesting Facts

Capital	**Population**
Basseterre	60,000
Official Language	**GDP**
English	$557 Million
Government	**Currency**
Unitary Parliamentary Republic	East Caribbean Dollar
Laws	**Driving**
Common Law	Left
Independence Day	**Internet**
September 19th, 1983	.kn
Total Area	**Calling Code**
261 Km2	+1 (869)

Nevis
Business Corporation

Introduction

A Nevis Business Corporation is a tax-free corporation designed to engage in all forms of international business with strict owner privacy laws, minimal record keeping and no reporting requirements. Suited for management consultants, network engineers, software developers, professionals traveling between countries on short-term assignments, internet based businesses, and international commodity trading, a Nevis Business Corporation may be used for a variety of international activities including use as a personal asset protection vehicle to passively hold property and investments. Under the Nevis Business Corporation Ordinance, such a corporation may be organized for most any lawful international business purpose or purposes. The Nevis Business Corporation Ordinance was first introduced in 1994 with tens of thousands of entities having been formed since that time.

Confidentiality and Privacy

St. Kitts & Nevis is an independent nation and has avoided entering any information sharing agreements with other countries in exchange for foreign aid. St. Kitts & Nevis is also not subject to the EU Savings Tax Directive as are some United Kingdom overseas territories. Unless a person is wanted for serious international crimes and is being investigated by the Financial Intelligence Unit for something like money laundering or INTERPOL suspects them for human trafficking, St. Kitts & Nevis does not share or report any information to overseas "principles" or organizations.

Nevis   Business Corporation

Company Laws	Nevis Business Corporation Ordinance, 1994
Official Document Language	English
Conduct Business Internationally	Yes
Conduct Business in Nevis	No
Resident Agent / Registered Office Required	Yes
Resident Secretary Required	No
Company Taxation	0 % of Worldwide Income
Double Taxation Avoidance Agreements	No
Company Tax Resident Qualification	No
Income Tax and Business Tax	No
Detailed Client Application Required	No
Minimum Shareholders	1
Company Shareholders Allowed	Yes
Residency of Shareholders Allowed	Non-Nevisian
Register of Shareholders	In Private Possession of Registered Agent
Register of Shareholders Public Record	No
Bearer Shares Permitted	Yes
Minimum Directors	1
Company Directors Allowed	Yes
Residency of Directors Allowed	Any Nationality
Register of Directors	In Private Possession of Registered Agent
Register of Directors Public Record	No
Disclosure of Beneficial Owners to Reg. Agent	Yes *(Due Diligence Requirements)*
Disclosure of Beneficial Owners with Registrar	No
Annual General Meeting Required	Yes
Shareholders / Directors Meeting Required	Yes *(Anywhere in the World or by Proxy)*
Company Minutes and Resolutions	In Private Possession of Registered Agent
Company Seal Required	No
Minimum Paid Up Capital Required	$0
Maximum Authorized Capital Investment	$100,000
Capital Considerations	Any Currency or in Kind
Subject to Currency Controls and Restrictions	No
Application Fees	No
Annual Government Fees	$235 First Year *($220 Thereafter)*
Keeping of Accounts Required	No
Filing of Accounts and Returns Required	No
Annual Government Return Filing Fees	No
Auditing of Accounts Required	No
Re-Domicile From or To a Foreign Country	Yes
Shelf Companies Available	Yes
Incorporation Time	1 Business Day

Government Licensing Fees

Regardless of the amount of authorized capital, paid up capital or total number of shares in a Nevis Business Corporation the annual government licensing fee is $220 (USD). The maximum authorized capital for such a Business Corporation is $100,000 (USD). In comparison to other tax havens, this flat annual licensing fee is very competitive.

Name Endings

Co	Company
Corp	Corporation
Inc	Incorporated
Ltd	Limited

Name Restrictions
Nevis Business Corporation Ordinance, 1994
Part IV - Formation of Corporations; Corporate Names (Section 22)

(1) Except as otherwise provided in subsection (2) of this section, the name of a corporation:
(ii) Shall not be the same as the name of a corporation of any type or kind, as such name appears on the index of names of existing corporations or companies or on the reserved name list maintained by the Registrar of Companies or a name so similar to any such name as to tend to confuse or deceive.

Rules of Operation
Nevis Business Corporation Ordinance, 1994
Part II - Corporate Purposes and Powers (Section 11)

Corporations may be organized under this Ordinance for any lawful business purpose or purposes.

Shares

A Nevis Business Corporation may issue shares in one or more classes, or one or more series within any class thereof, any or all of which classes may be of shares with:

1.) Bearer
2.) No Par Value
3.) Non-Voting
4.) Par Value

5.) Registered
6.) Voting (Full or Limited)
7.) Shares with such designations, preferences and relative, participating, optional, or special rights and qualifications, limitations, or restrictions thereon.

Bearer Shares

Nevis Business Corporation Ordinance, 1994
Part V - Corporate Finance (Section 31)

(1) *. . . Provided that any share certificate issued to a bearer share shall not be distributed but shall be retained in the safe custody of the registered agent for the corporation which issued such certificate is in the safe custody of any other person authorized by the Minister from time to time as an approved custodian of any such bearer share certificate . . .*

Taxation

By legal definition, a Nevis Business Corporation and its shareholders are not subject to any Nevis tax or duty derived from income or profits, stamp duties on all transfers of property, transactions of shares, debt obligations and other securities.

Nevis Business Corporation Ordinance, 1994
Part XIV - Tax Exemption (Section 123)

(1) *Any corporation subject to this Ordinance which does no business in Nevis shall not be subject to any corporate tax, income tax, withholding tax, stamp tax, asset tax, exchange controls, or other fees or taxes based upon or measured by assets or income originating outside of Nevis or in connection with other activities outside of Nevis or in connection with matters of corporate administration which may occur in Nevis, except as provided in sections 6 and 7 of Part 1 of this Ordinance.*

(2) *For purposes of this section, no corporation shall be considered to be doing business in. Nevis solely because it engages in one or more of the following activities:*
- *(i)   maintaining bank accounts in Nevis:*
- *(ii)   holding meetings of directors or shareholders in Nevis:*
- *(iii) maintaining corporate or financial records in Nevis:*
- *(iv) maintaining an administrative or managerial office in Nevis with respect to assets or activities outside of Nevis:*
- *(v)   maintaining a registered agent in Nevis: and*
- *(vi) investing in stocks or entities of Nevis corporations or being a partner in Nevis partnership or a beneficiary of a Nevis trust or estate*
- *(vii) acquires real property in a local industrial or tourist facility provided always that such property*
- *(viii) shall be situated in a project or development approved and authorized by the Nevis Island Administration.*

St Kitts & Nevis
Foundation

Introduction

Over 60% of the world is under a form of civil law government including most of Europe and all of Asia, with the exception of Hong Kong and Singapore. Foundations are widely excepted in the international community and preferred in most countries operating under civil law. A St Kitts & Nevis Foundation is a separate legal entity just like a company, but has beneficiaries rather than shareholders. Assets transferred to a foundation become the property of the foundation with full legal and beneficial title and are no longer the assets of the founder. Once a foundation has been funded it is managed by a foundation council for the directing of investments and appointment and removal of councillors, protectors and beneficiaries. The foundation council is located in St Kitts & Nevis, which is a nil tax jurisdiction, and mitigates potential tax risks from aggressive taxing authorities in other countries.

St. Kitts & Nevis   Foundation

Foundation Laws	Foundations Act, 2003
Official Document Language	English
Conduct Business Internationally	Yes
Conduct Business in St. Kitts & Nevis	Yes
Resident Agent Required	Yes *(Foundation Service Provider)*
Registered Office Required	Yes *(Foundation Service Provider)*
Resident Secretary Required	Yes *(Individual or Entity)*
Company Taxation	0 % of Worldwide Income
Double Taxation Avoidance Agreements	No
Company Tax Resident Qualification	No
Income Tax and Business Tax	No
Detailed Client Application Required	No
Minimum Founders	1
Company Founders Allowed	Yes
Residency of Founders Allowed	Non-Nevisian
Register of Founders	In Private Possession of Registered Agent
Register of Founders Public Record	Yes *(Nominee Founders Permitted)*
Minimum Councillors	1
Company Councillors Allowed	Yes
Residency of Councillors Allowed	Any Nationality
Register of Councillors	In Private Possession of Registered Agent
Register of Councillors Public Record	No
Disclosure of Beneficiaries to Reg. Agent	Yes *(Due Diligence Requirements)*
Disclosure of Beneficiaries with Registrar	No
Annual General Meeting Required	Yes *(Anywhere in the World or by Proxy)*
Foundation Minutes and Resolutions	In Private Possession of Registered Agent
Minimum Funding	$1
Capital Considerations	Any Currency or in Kind
Subject to Currency Controls and Restrictions	No
Application Fees	No
Annual Government Fees	$235 First Year *($220 Thereafter)*
Keeping of Accounts Required	Yes
Filing of Accounts and Returns Required	No
Annual Government Return Filing Fees	No
Auditing of Accounts Required	No
Re-Domicile from a Foreign Country	Yes
Re-Domicile to a Foreign Country	Yes
Shelf Foundations Available	Yes
Incorporation Time	1 Business Day

Books and Records

Foundations Act, 2003
Part V - Accounts and Audit (Section 22 - Accounts)

(2) A Foundation shall cause to be kept proper books of account with respect to —
(a) all sums of money received, expended and distributed by the Foundation and the matters in respect of which the receipt, expenditure and distribution takes place;
(b) all sales and purchases by the Foundation; and
(c) the assets and liabilities of the Foundation.

Foundation

Founder

The founder is the person who is creating the foundation and may be any individual, legal entity or nominee. St. Kitts & Nevis foundations permit two or more co-founders. A founder, or another person assigned the rights of the founder in the Charter or Regulations, may reserve special rights to direct investments, appoint and remove beneficiaries, or even dissolve the foundation. A founder may even be the sole beneficiary of the foundation during his lifetime, so long as successors are appointed.

Councillor

The councillor manages the business affairs of the foundation and may be natural individuals or legal entities. A minimum of one councillor is required. Councillors may be of any nationality and reside anywhere in the world. A founder may be councillor, but not the sole councillor.

Guardian

A guardian is the person who oversees the trustee and activities of the trust. The foundation may appoint a guardian if provisioned in the Charter or Regulations. A sole councillor or sole beneficiary may not act as a guardian.

Beneficiary

Beneficiaries receive the distribution of assets according the Charter or Regulations. However, beneficiaries of a St. Kitts & Nevis foundation are not owners and have no rights or control over the assets belonging to the foundation.

Funding

A St. Kitts & Nevis Foundation must have initial assets of $1 minimum. Assets may originate from any lawful source either from the founder or a third party and may consist of present or future assets of any nature.

Government Licensing Fees

Annual government licensing fees are $235 in year one, then $220 thereafter due annually upon the original registration date.

Names

The name may be in any language, but if the name is other than English it must be accompanied with the respective language translation.

Name Endings

Foundation

Regulations

A foundation may adopt a document entitled Regulations, which is private and not filed with the registry. The Regulations may, for example, provide for the identification and designation of councillors, beneficiaries, distribution of the foundation assets and beneficiary entitlement proportions.

Rules of Operation

A St. Kitts & Nevis Foundation is created for the management and distribution of assets in accordance with the Charter or Regulations for the purpose of either family succession as a "private foundation", for charitable causes as a "charity foundation", for a specified reason as a "purpose foundation" or any combinations of the three.

Taxation

Income and distributions to beneficiaries are completely exempt from taxation in St. Kitts & Nevis even if "managed and controlled" by a Foundation Council from St. Kitts & Nevis.

Nevis
International Exempt Trust

Introduction

A Nevis International Exempt Trust is an irrevocable trust established generally in perpetuity of 100 years. Nevis Courts have jurisdiction for all matters relating to a Nevis International Exempt Trust and any transfers of property into the trust may not be voided or invalidated due to any foreign rule of forced heirship. A Nevis International Exempt Trust will also remain in full effect even if the trust concept is not recognized or admitted under the laws of a foreign jurisdiction.

Nevis   International Exempt Trust

Trust Laws	Nevis International Exempt Trust Ordinance
Official Document Language	English
Resident Agent Required	Yes
Registered Office Required	Yes
Resident Secretary Required	No
Trust Taxation	0 % of Worldwide Income
Double Taxation Avoidance Agreements	No
Income Tax and Business Tax	No
Detailed Client Application Required	No
Minimum Settlors	1
Company Settlors Allowed	Yes
Residency of Settlors Allowed	Non-Nevisian
Register of Settlors	In Private Possession of Registered Agent
Register of Settlors Public Record	No
Minimum Trustees	2 *(Only 1 if a Company Trustee)*
Company Trustees Allowed	Yes
Residency of Trustees Allowed	Yes *(International Trust Service Provider)*
Register of Trustees	In Private Possession of Registered Agent
Register of Trustees Public Record	No
Company Protectors Allowed	Yes
Disclosure of Beneficiaries to Reg. Agent	Yes *(Due Diligence Requirements)*
Disclosure of Beneficiaries with Registrar	No
Annual General Meeting Required	No
Minimum Funding	$1
Capital Considerations	Any Currency or in Kind
Subject to Currency Controls and Restrictions	No
Application Fees	$235 First Year *($220 Thereafter)*
Annual Government Fees	No
Keeping of Accounts Required	Yes
Filing of Accounts and Returns Required	No
Annual Government Return Filing Fees	No
Auditing of Accounts Required	No
Re-Domicile from a Foreign Country	Yes
Re-Domicile to a Foreign Country	Yes
Shelf Trusts Available	No
Registration Time	1 Business Day

Books and Records

A Nevis International Exempt Trust is required to maintain accounting records.

Funding

A Nevis International Exempt Trust may include anything not specifically mentioned in the Nevis International Exempt Trust Regulations.

Nevis International Exempt Trust Ordinance, 1994
Part 9 - Miscellaneous
Section 45 - Investments

(1) A trustee shall not invest any of the trust funds other than in securities, assets, or property authorized expressly or by necessary implication for the investment of the trust funds by and under the instrument by which the trust is established or created.

(2) Where the instrument by which the trust is created or established authorizes expressly or by necessary implication the investment of the trust funds in any investments authorized by the laws of St. Christopher and Nevis for the investment of trust funds the instrument shall be deemed to authorize investment as Schedule expressed in the Schedule to this Ordinance.

Government Licensing Fees

Annual government licensing fees are $235 in year one, then $220 thereafter due annually upon the original registration date.

Names

The Trust Deed is a private document and not filed publicly and may therefore be named in any manner desired. Generally, the type of trust is listed in the trust name.

Name Endings

Charitable Trust
Common Trust
International Exempt Trust
Protective Trust
Purpose Trust
Spendthrift Trust
Unit Trust

Rules of Operation

A Nevis International Exempt Trust is created for the management and distribution of assets in accordance with the trust agreement for the purpose of estate planning and family succession, charitable causes as in a charitable trust or other specified reasons as in a purpose trust.

Taxation

A Nevis International Exempt Trust is completely exempt from business tax, withholding tax, capital gains tax and stamp duty in St. Kitts & Nevis.

Trust

Settlor

A settlor is the person who created the trust. A settlor of a Nevis International Exempt Trust may be an individual or a legal entity. A settlor may not be a resident of St. Kitts & Nevis at any time during the existence of the trust.

Trustee

A trustee is the person who holds and disburses the assets of the trust. A Nevis International Exempt Trust permits a trustee to be an individual or legal entity residing absolutely anywhere in the world. At all times the must be at least one St. Kitts & Nevis resident trustee who is a licensed International Trustee Service Provider. A settlor may be a trustee, but not the sole trustee.

Protector

A protector, sometimes known as a compliance enforcer, is the person who oversees the trustee and activities of the trust. The appointment of a protector must be provided for in the Trust Deed. A protector is generally given powers for the appointment and removal of trustees. The rights for a Protector to amend the Trust Deed must be clearly indicated in the Deed.

Beneficiary
Nevis International Exempt Trust Ordinance, 1994
Part 6 - Trustees, Protectors and Beneficiaries
Section 32 - Beneficiaries of Trusts

(1) *A beneficiary shall be -*
    (a) *identifiable by name; or*
    (b) *ascertainable by reference to -*
        (i) *a class; or*
        (ii) *a relationship to some person, whether or not living at the time of the creation of the trust or at the time which under the terms of the trust is the time by reference to which members of a class are to be determined.*

Nevis
Limited Liability Company

Introduction

Members of a Nevis Limited Liability Company (LLC) have a 'limited' amount of liability and are liable only up to the amount of their capital contribution to the company. Since an LLC is a flow-through entity, members may be responsible for filing an annual return in their tax resident jurisdiction reflecting their respective financial involvement in the LLC. Provided no business is conducted within Nevis, there are no Nevis tax liabilities. A properly structured offshore Limited Liability Company aids in enhancing anonymity, provides outstanding asset protection benefits from judgement creditors, and may reduce or eliminate various tax liabilities.

Nevis   Limited Liability Company

Company Laws	Limited Liability Company Ordinance, 1995
Official Document Language	English
Conduct Business Internationally	Yes
Conduct Business in Nevis	Yes
Resident Agent Required	Yes
Registered Office Required	Yes
Resident Secretary Required	No
Company Taxation	Fiscally Transparent *(Tax Flow-Through)*
Double Taxation Avoidance Agreements	No
Company Tax Resident Qualification	No
Income Tax and Business Tax	No
Detailed Client Application Required	No
Minimum Members	1
Corporate Members Allowed	Yes
Residency of Members Allowed	Any Nationality
Register of Members	Yes
Register of Members Public Record	Yes
Disclosure of Beneficial Owners to Reg. Agent	Yes *(Due Diligence Requirements)*
Disclosure of Beneficial Owners with Registrar	No *(Not if Members are Offshore Entities)*
Annual General Meeting Required	No
Members Meeting Required	Yes *(Anywhere in the World or by Proxy)*
Company Minutes and Resolutions	Yes
Company Seal Required	No
Minimum Paid Up Capital Required	$0
Maximum Authorized Capital Investment	$100,000
Capital Considerations	Any Currency or in Kind
Subject to Currency Controls and Restrictions	No
Application Fees	No
Annual Government Fees	$235 First Year *($220 Thereafter)*
Keeping of Accounts Required	No
Filing of Accounts and Returns Required	No
Annual Government Return Filing Fees	No
Auditing of Accounts Required	No
Re-Domicile from a Foreign Country	Yes
Re-Domicile to a Foreign Country	Yes
Shelf Companies Available	Yes
Incorporation Time	1 Business Day

Government Licensing Fees

Regardless of the amount of authorized capital, paid up capital or total number of shares in a Nevis Limited Liability Company the annual government licensing fee is $220 (USD). The maximum authorized capital for such an LLC is $100,000 (USD). In comparison to other tax havens, this flat annual licensing fee is very competitive.

Membership Interests

Nevis Limited Liability Company Ordinance, 1995
Part VII - Members and Members' Interests
Section 39 - Classes and Series of Members Interests

(1) *Members' interest in a limited liability company may be: series of member's interest*
  (a)   of one or more classes or one or more series within any class thereof;
  (b)   with voting powers, full or limited, or without voting powers;
  (c)   and with such designations, preferences, rights, qualifications, limitations or restrictions thereon as shall be stated in the operating agreement.
(2) *A limited liability company may provide in its operating agreement for one or more classes or series of members' interest which are redeemable, in whole or in part, at the option of the limited liability company at such price or prices, within such period and under such conditions as are stated in the operating agreement.*

Name Endings

LC	Limited Liability Company
LLC	Limited Liability Company

Name Restrictions

Nevis Limited Liability Company Ordinance, 1995
Part V - Formation of Limited Liability Companies;
Names; Amendment of Articles of Organization (Section 23 - Company Name)

(1) *Except as otherwise provided in Subsection (2) of this section, the name of the limited liability company:*
  (b)   Shall not be the same as the name of a limited liability company or of any other company of any type or kind, as such name appears on the index of names of existing limited liability companies or companies or on the reserved name list maintained by the Registrar of Companies or a name so similar to any such name as to tend to confuse or deceive.

Rules of Operation

Nevis Limited Liability Company Ordinance, 1995
Part II - Purposes and Powers (Section 12 - Purposes)

(12) Limited liability companies may be organized under this Ordinance for any lawful business purpose or purposes, including, without limitation, the rendering of professional services by or through its members, managers, officers or agents, subject to any licensing or registration requirements applicable in any jurisdiction in which the services are rendered or in which such persons are licensed or registered.

Taxation

By legal definition, a Nevis Limited Liability Company and its members are not subject to any tax or duty derived from income or profits, stamp duties on all transfers of property, transactions of shares, debt obligations and other securities.

Nevis Limited Liability Company Ordinance, 1995
Part XV - Tax Exemption (Section 83 - Exemption)

(1) Any limited liability company subject to this Ordinance which does no business in Nevis shall not be subject to any corporate tax, income tax, withholding tax, stamp tax, asset tax, exchange controls, or other fees or taxes based upon or measured by assets or income originating outside of Nevis or in connection with other activities outside of Nevis or in connection with matters of corporate administration which may occur in Nevis, except as provided in sections 6 and 7.

(2) For purposes of this section, no limited liability company shall be considered to be doing business in Nevis solely because it engages in one or more of the following activities:
(a) maintaining bank accounts in Nevis;
(b) holding meetings of managers or members in Nevis;
(c) maintaining company or financial records in Nevis;
(d) maintaining an administrative or managerial office in Nevis with respect to assets or activities outside of Nevis;
(e) maintaining a registered agent in Nevis;
(f) investing in stocks or interests of Nevis corporations or limited liability companies or being a partner in a Nevis partnership or a beneficiary of a Nevis trust or estate.

United Kingdom

About the United Kingdom

Activities

London alone offers an array of activities for tourists and residents alike. Double-decker city bus tours, Thames River cruise, the London Eye, Tower of London, the Crown Jewels, St. Paul's Cathedral, Buckingham Palace Park, Westminster Abbey, Houses of Parliament and depending on the time of year - the changing of the guard. Within the United Kingdom there are literally hundreds of castles available for viewing, some have even been restored and converted into luxury hotels. Some of the more famous castles are Arundel, Blarney, Bodium, Dover, Edinburgh, Leeds, Rochester, Warwick and of course Windsor. Other highlights within the UK include the Salisbury Cathedral, Loch Ness (Monster), Stonehenge, the Georgian Baths, Oxford and Cambridge Campuses, London Zoo, Albert Hall and White Cliffs of Dover.

Climate

The UK has a damp oceanic climate. Depending on the location, temperatures may range from -10°C in the winter to 30°C in the summer with annual rainfall easily exceeding 2 meters. Winter seasons are very long and known to be gray and dreary lasting from November through the end of March, sometimes into April. It is not uncommon to see as little as 24 to 30 hours of total sunshine during the course of a winter month. Generally, weather in the UK is cooler with higher levels of precipitation to the North and West with a slightly warmer, dryer climate to the South and East. The summer months of July and August are considered the most desirable time of year with long sunny days, mild afternoon showers and temperatures of 16° to 17°C.

Culture

Cultural influences of the United Kingdom extend well past England, Scotland, Wales and Northern Ireland into Canada, Australia, New Zealand, South Africa, India, Pakistan, the United States and all 14 nations comprising the Overseas Territories. The industrial revolution is attributed to the UK inciting changes in agriculture, manufacturing and transportation. UK art, architecture, literature, poetry, music, theatre, television and cinema have all impacted the global consciousness. The United Kingdom is abound with museums, galleries and libraries.

People from around the world travel to the UK to study science, mathematics, technology, religion, philosophy, politics, cuisine, sports medicine, fashion and business management.

Economy and Offshore Financial Services

London is considered to be one of the largest financial centers in the world and has lead the British economy to become one of the most globalized on the planet. After Germany and France, the UK has the 3rd largest economy in Europe and 6th largest in the world. Banking, insurance and business services account for the largest portion of the nation's Gross Domestic Product (GDP). Agriculture commodities include cereals, oilseed, potatoes, vegetables, cattle, sheep, poultry and fish. Industrial commodities include machine tools, shipbuilding, aircraft, motor vehicles and parts, electronics and communications equipment, metals, chemicals, coal, petroleum, paper products, food processing and clothing as well as electric power, automation and railroad equipment. Taxation in the United Kingdom is very high in the form income tax, national insurance, Value Added Tax (VAT), corporate tax and fuel duty. According to Her Majesties (HM) Treasury, tax as a percentage of GDP reached 46% as of 2005-2006. Asset Protection Services of America offers incorporation services for UK Limited Liability Partnerships.

Geography

The United Kingdom (UK) is located between the North Atlantic Ocean and the North Sea and comprises Great Britain (England, Scotland, Wales) and Northern Ireland. England accounts for more than half of the overall landmass and is separated from France by only 35 kilometers of water in the English Channel. The UK has a fault-line running through the center of it separating the highlands to the North and West from the lowlands to the South and East. The terrain is primarily composed of ancient volcanic rocks, limestone, sandstone and shale. The highest point is Ben Nevis in Scotland towering at 1,344 meters above sea level with the lowest point being in the Fens of East Anglia in England reaching a depth of 4 meters below sea level. The River Severn is the longest river stretching 354 kilometers through England and Wales. The coastline of the UK spans 12,429 kilometers.

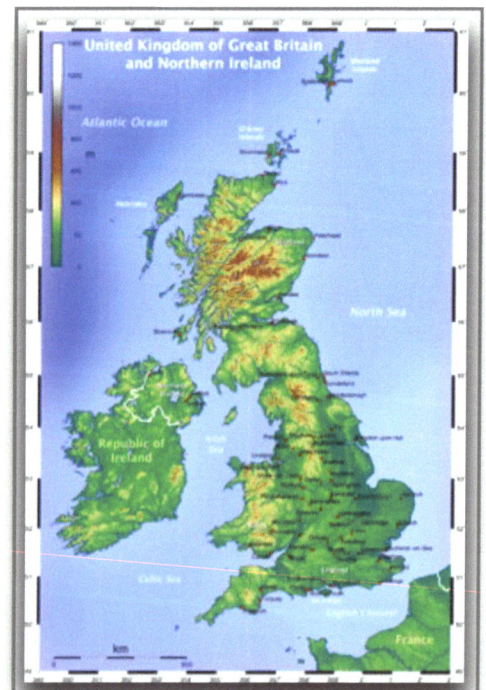

History

The Kingdom of England (included Wales) and the Kingdom of Scotland were formerly separate states. On May 1, 1707 the United Kingdom of Great Britain was formed in accordance with the Treaty of Union joining the Kingdoms by sharing a single constitutional monarch and parliament. The Act of Union in 1800 added the Kingdom of Ireland to create the United Kingdom of Great Britain and Ireland. After nearly a century of struggle for global control the "British Empire" had at the height of its power dominion over nearly a half a billion people totaling one quarter of the world's population. In 1922 Ireland seceded under the Anglo-Irish Treaty and became a free state for one day. Northern Ireland immediately seceded from the Irish free state the next day and rejoined the United Kingdom. In 1927 the formal UK title became "The United Kingdom of Great Britain and Northern Ireland". After World War II most of the countries formerly under the control of the United Kingdom joined the Commonwealth of Nations, an intergovernmental organization of 54 individual member states. 14 countries chose to retain the British monarch as their head of state and became independent sovereign states. Since 2002 those 14 nations have been known as British Overseas Territories. The United Kingdom is currently a leading member of the United Nations, the European Union and NATO.

Interesting Facts

Capital	**Population**
London	52,000,000
Official Language	**GDP**
English	$41.9 Trillion
Government	**Currency**
Monarchy	£ Great British Pound
Laws	**Driving**
Common Law	Left
Independence Day	**Internet**
April 21st (Queen's Birthday)	.gb
Total Area	**Calling Code**
245,000 Km2	+44

United Kingdom
Limited Liability Company (LLP)

Introduction

A United Kingdom Limited Liability Partnership (LLP) was established on the 9th of January in 2009. Traditionally, in a limited partnership, the general partner has unlimited liability for the debts and obligations of the partnership. However in this new legislation for a Limited Liability Partnership there are a minimum of two partners each with a 'limited' amount of liability. And the partners in a United Kingdom Limited Liability Partnership are liable only up to the amount of their contribution to the partnership. Since an LLP is a flow-through entity, each partner is responsible for filing an annual tax return reflecting their respective financial involvement with the LLP. Provided no business is conducted with or within the United Kingdom or by a UK resident, there are no United Kingdom tax liabilities. And utilizing entities properly structured offshore as the partners of the LLP not only aids in enhancing anonymity and asset protection benefits, it may eliminate any tax liability for citizens outside the United Kingdom who wish to have their business headquartered in Europe.

United Kingdom   Limited Liability Partnership (LLP)

Partnership Laws	Limited Liability Partnerships Act, 2000
	Income and Corporation Taxes Act, 1998
Official Document Language	English
Conduct Business Internationally	Yes
Conduct Business in Seychelles	Yes
Resident Agent / Registered Office Required	Yes
Resident Secretary Required	No
Company Taxation	Fiscally Transparent *(Taxes Flow to Partners)*
Double Taxation Avoidance Agreements	No
Company Tax Resident Qualification	Yes
Income Tax and Business Tax	Yes
Detailed Client Application Required	No
Minimum Partners	2
Corporate Partners Allowed	Yes
Residency of Partners Allowed	Any Nationality
Register of Partners	Yes
Register of Partners Public Record	Yes
Disclosure of Beneficial Owners to Reg. Agent	Yes *(Due Diligence Requirements)*
Disclosure of Beneficial Owners with Registrar	No *(Not if Partners are Offshore Entities)*
Annual General Meeting Required	No
Partners Meeting Required	Yes *(Anywhere in the World or by Proxy)*
Partnership Minutes and Resolutions	Yes
Partnership Seal Required	No
Minimum Paid Up Capital Required	£ 2 *(Great British Pounds)*
Maximum Authorized Capital Investment	*(Not Applicable)*
Capital Considerations	Any Currency or in Kind
Subject to Currency Controls and Restrictions	No
Application Fees	No
Annual Government Fees	£ 0 *(Great British Pounds)*
Keeping of Accounts Required	Yes
Filing of Accounts and Returns Required	Yes
Annual Government Return Filing Fees	Yes
Auditing of Accounts Required	Yes
Re-Domicile from a Foreign Country	Yes
Re-Domicile to a Foreign Country	Yes
Shelf Partnerships Available	No
Incorporation Time	1 Business Day

Paid Up Capital

The minimum Paid Up Capital for a UK Limited Liability Partnership is £2 (GBP).

Confidentiality and Privacy

There are no inherent privacy or confidentiality benefits in a United Kingdom Limited Liability Partnership. In fact, the entity is virtually transparent both from an ownership and tax perspective. The benefits of using a UK LLP arise from incorporating offshore Seychelles International Business Companies (IBC) for the two required partners. In this regard, it is the Republic of Seychelles which is providing the privacy, confidentiality and tax savings for the owner(s) of the United Kingdom LLP.

Financial Reporting

A UK Limited Liability Partnership is required to prepare and file annual financial accounts and may be subject to audits. The partnership is free to arrange its business accounts in any manner fitting to establish and maintain reasonable accuracy of the partnership's financial position.

Government Licensing Fees

There are no annual licensing fees (£0 GBP) for a United Kingdom Limited Liability Partnership.

United Kingdom Limited Liability Partnerships Act, 2000
Chapter 12
Part - Incorporation
Section 2 - Incorporation Documentation

(2) The incorporation document must—
- *(a) be in a form approved by the registrar (or as near to such a form as circumstances allow),*
- *(b) state the name of the limited liability partnership,*
- *(c) state whether the registered office of the limited liability partnership is to be situated in England and Wales, in Wales or in Scotland,*
- *(d) state the address of that registered office,*
- *(e) state the name and address of each of the persons who are to be members of the limited liability partnership on incorporation, and*
- *(f) either specify which of those persons are to be designated members or state that every person who from time to time is a member of the limited liability partnership is a designated member.*

Name Endings

LLP	Limited Liability Partnership
PAC	Partneriaeth Atebolrwydd Cyfyngedig

Name Restrictions

United Kingdom Limited Liability Partnerships Act, 2000
Chapter 12
Schedule - Names and Registered Offices
Part 1 - Names (Section 3 - Registration of Names)

(1) *A limited liability partnership shall not be registered by a name—*
- *(a)* *which includes, otherwise than at the end of the name, either of the expressions "limited liability partnership" and "partneriaeth atebolrwydd cyfyngedig" or any of the abbreviations "llp", "LLP", "pac" and "PAC",*
- *(b)* *which is the same as a name appearing in the index kept under section 714(1) of the M16Companies Act 1985,*
- *(c)* *the use of which by the limited liability partnership would in the opinion of the Secretary of State constitute a criminal offence, or*
- *(d)* *which in the opinion of the Secretary of State is offensive.*

(2) *Except with the approval of the Secretary of State, a limited liability partnership shall not be registered by a name which—*
- *(a)* *in the opinion of the Secretary of State would be likely to give the impression that it is connected in any way with Her Majesty's Government or with any local authority, or Limited Liability Partnerships Act, 2000*
- *(b)* *includes any word or expression for the time being specified in regulations under section 29 of the M17Companies Act 1985 (names needing approval), and in paragraph (a) "local authority" means any local authority within the meaning of the M18Local Government Act 1972 or the M19Local Government etc. (Scotland) Act 1994, the Common Council of the City of London or the Council of the Isles of Scilly.*

Partnership Interests

Partnership interests are equal, unless otherwise prescribed in writing by agreement between the members.

United Kingdom Limited Liability Partnerships Act, 2000
Chapter 12
Part - Membership (Section 5 - Relationship of Members)

(1) *Except as far as otherwise provided by this Act or any other enactment, the mutual rights and duties of the members of a limited liability partnership, and the mutual rights and duties of a limited liability partnership and its members, shall be governed—*
  (a)   by agreement between the members, or between the limited liability partnership and its members, or
  (b)   in the absence of agreement as to any matter, by any provision made in relation to that matter by regulations under section 15(c).
(2) *An agreement made before the incorporation of a limited liability partnership between the persons who subscribe their names to the incorporation document may impose obligations on the limited liability partnership (to take effect at any time after its incorporation).*

Rules of Operation

Non-Profit Organizations may not use a UK Limited Liability Partnership as a company structure. There are also some restricted businesses including banking, insurance, financial services, consumer credit related services and employment agencies. Otherwise, any trade or profession may may utilize a United Kingdom Limited Liability Partnership for its business operations.

Taxation

A UK Limited Liability Partnership is a flow-through tax entity and not liable for taxation on profits or gains arising from within the partnership. The partners are liable to file their own respective tax returns but are exempt from UK tax provided that no business or trade is conducted with, or within, the United Kingdom. For more information on the taxation of a UK Limited Liability Partnership please see Section 118 of the Income and Corporation Taxes Act, 1988.

U.S. Offshore
Tax Filing Requirements

Classification of Taxpayers for U.S. Tax Purposes

U.S. law treats U.S. persons and foreign persons differently for tax purposes. Therefore, it is important to be able to distinguish between these two types of taxpayers.

United States Persons

The term 'United States person' means and includes:

- ✓ A citizen or resident alien of the United States
- ✓ A domestic partnership
- ✓ A domestic corporation
- ✓ Any estate other than a foreign estate
- ✓ Any trust if:
  - – A court within the United States is able to exercise primary supervision over the administration of the trust, and
  - – One or more United States persons have the authority to control all substantial decisions of the trust
- ✓ Any other person that is not a foreign person.

Foreign Persons

A foreign person includes:

- ✓ Nonresident alien individual
- ✓ Foreign corporation
- ✓ Foreign partnership
- ✓ Foreign trust
- ✓ A foreign estate
- ✓ Any other person that is not a U.S. person

Generally, the U.S. branch of a foreign corporation or partnership is treated as a foreign person.

See Check-the-box Entities (Form 8832 and Instructions)

For Federal tax purposes, certain business entities automatically are classified as corporations. Except for a business entity automatically classified as a corporation, a business entity with at least two members can choose to be classified as either an association taxable as a corporation or a partnership, and a business entity with a single member can choose to be classified as either an association taxable as a corporation or disregarded as an entity separate from its owner. Other business entities may choose how they are classified for Federal tax purposes.

IRS Form 926

U.S. Persons, domestic corporations, domestic estates or trusts are required to annually file Form 926 Return by a U.S. Transferor of Property to a Foreign Corporation to report any exchanges or transfers of property described in section 6038B(a)(1)(A) to a foreign corporation.

The U.S. transferor must file the Form 926 and the additional information required under Regulations section 1.6038B-1(c) and Temporary Regulations sections 1. 6038B-1T(c) (1) through (5) and 1.6038B-1T(d) with their income tax return for the tax year that includes the date of the transfer.

The person could be subject to a penalty for failure to file equaling 10% of the fair market value of the property at the time of the exchange/transfer if the taxpayer fails to comply with the filing requirement. The penalty will not apply if the failure to comply is due to reasonable cause and not willful neglect. The penalty is limited to $100,000 unless the failure to comply was due to intentional disregard. Moreover, the period of limitations for assessment of tax upon the exchange/transfer of that property is extended to the date that is 3 years after the date on which the information required to be reported is provided.

IRS Form 5471

The Internal Revenue Service (IRS) reminds taxpayers that U.S. citizens and U.S. residents who are officers, directors or shareholders in foreign corporations are responsible for filing IRS Form 5471 Information Return of U.S. Persons With Respect to Certain Foreign Corporations.

The form and attached schedules are used to satisfy the reporting requirements under Sections 6038 and 6046 of the Internal Revenue Code. Substantial penalties exist for U.S. citizens and U.S. residents who are liable for filing Form 5471 and who fail to do so.

The categories of persons potentially liable for filing Form 5471 include U.S. citizens, resident alien individuals, U.S. domestic corporations, U.S. domestic partnerships and U.S. domestic trusts. The filing requirements for Form 5471 relate to persons who have a certain level of control in foreign corporations as described on pages 1-3 of the Instructions for Form 5471.

Please refer to those instructions for the details about who is liable for filing Form 5471, as form 5471 should be filed as an attachment (or electronically) to the taxpayer's federal income tax return with a duplicate copy being filed with the IRS Center in Philadelphia.

Report of Foreign Bank and Financial Accounts
TD F 90-22.1 Report of Foreign Bank and Financial Accounts

Who Must Use This Form?

Any foreign financial accounts with an aggregate account balance reaching or exceeding $10,000 during a calendar year must file this form. The form is due on June 30th of the year following the taxable year of the taxpayer and should be sent to the U.S. Department of the Treasury, P.O. Box 32621, Detroit, MI 48232-0621.

What Constitutes a Foreign Financial Account?

Generally, a foreign financial account includes a bank account, savings account, money market fund, demand deposit, securities account or similar account. There are a few exceptions, but any US person who may have any possible obligation to file this form should carefully read the instructions to the form.

What is a 'Financial Interest'?

"Financial Interest" includes interests in Foreign Accounts titled in the names of nominees, agents and trusts (if the beneficial interest in the trust exceeds 50% in corpus or income).

What is a 'Signature Authority'?

"Signature Authority" includes control of the disposition of the Foreign Account by oral or written instructions to the signatory or titleholder on the account.

Who May Be Required to File the Form?

This form **may be** required to be filed by those who are shareholders, officers or directors of foreign corporations, partners in foreign partnerships, grantors of foreign trusts or beneficiaries of foreign estates or trusts. In some arrangements, a trust account is set up offshore, requiring the signature of both the trustee and a trust protector to facilitate withdrawals. In such instances, the trust protector may have an obligation to file the Form TD F 90-22.1.

Policy owners of foreign fixed return annuity or life insurance contracts will not have any authority over, or beneficial interest in, the management of the cash values in the policy. However, even though a policy owner of a variable annuity or variable life policy may not have any direct authority over the investments in the segregated account, the policy owner has a beneficial interest in the segregated account and should file this form to disclose such an interest.

Can Tangible Assets in the U.S. be Transferred Offshore Without Reporting?

Such transfers by a transferor **may not** be required to be reported if, again, the aggregate amount does not reach or exceed $10,000 (in any combined accounts) during a calendar year. However, if assets are gifted to another person, or if the transferor dies with those assets, he or she may be subject to gift tax or estate tax since domiciliaries in the U.S. are taxed on worldwide assets including transfers during one's lifetime or at death.

Can You Transfer Certificates Offshore Without Reporting?

A certificate (of ownership) of precious metals is personal property, not the underlying hard metal. If certificates are transferred offshore it would appears to be the same as the transfer of any other intangible asset such as a share of stock, partnership interest or membership interest in a limited liability company, etc. If certificates of precious metals are transferred to a safe deposit box in a foreign bank, this safe deposit box appears to be classified as a "foreign account" because the safe deposit box is registered in the name of the certificate holder. Valuables or documents purchased outside the U.S. and placed directly into a non-U.S. safe deposit box or private vault apparently do not constitute a foreign account since private vaults are not private institutions.

What Information Is Required?

The form requires taxpayer identification information (name, address, TIN, etc.) and the number of the foreign financial accounts. For each financial account, the form requests a description of the type of account, the range of value in the account, the account number, the name of the institution, the country where the account is located and the name of the organization (corporation, partnership, trust or estate). The exact filing requirements are provided in the instructions to the form.

How Long Does It Take To Prepare?

For those with a single foreign financial account, it may take less than 15 minutes to complete the form. Additional time will be required for each additional financial account.

What are the Penalties for Failure to Comply?

According to the instructions to the form, "Civil and criminal penalties, including in certain circumstances a fine of not more than $500,000 and imprisonment of not more than five years, are provided for failure to file a report, supply information, and for filing a false or fraudulent report." (31 CFR 103).

RESOLUTION OF
(Replace This With The Name Of Your Corp)
A *(Name of Country)* CORPORATION
TO
UNDERTAKE INTERNATIONAL INVESTING AND
ESTABLISHING THE AUTHORIZED SIGNATORY FOR SAID INVESTING

The Secretary announced that pursuant to the Articles of Incorporation and/or Bylaws of the above named Corporation, a special meeting of the Directors was held on the _____ day of _____, 20____ at _____ o'clock __M. The chairman then declared that the meeting was to be held in compliance with applicable statutes.

The chairman of the meeting then discussed the company's intention to undertake international investments directly from the funds of this company, or by engaging the services of an international company, or by creating a suitable international company for said purposes.

The chairman of the meeting then discussed granting full signatory authority to the named Authorized Signatory to sign all necessary instruments, contracts, banking documents and any other documents on behalf of this corporation that may be required to further the purposes of this company.

On motion duly made and carried, it was, **RESOLVED** and **ORDERED** that the named Authorized Signatory be henceforth granted the full signatory authority and power to directly utilize the funds of this company to execute agreements, leases, banking documents and/or other instrument(s) necessary to undertake any type of international investments deemed appropriate on behalf of this company; or to contract and pay for the services of an international company to undertake investments deemed appropriate on behalf of this company; or to create a suitable international company on behalf of the above mentioned company for said purposes.

Additionally the named Authorized Signatory was authorized to execute any and all documents deemed necessary to further the purposes summarized herein, without the attestation of the Board of Directors or affixing of the corporate seal thereto and upon execution of such instruments by the named Authorized Signatory, such documents so executed shall be valid and binding without further act or specific resolution of any kind whatsoever.

UNDERTAKE INTERNATIONAL INVESTING AND ESTABLISHING THE AUTHORIZED SIGNATORY FOR SAID INVESTING

CERTIFICATION OF CORPORATE SECRETARY

I the undersigned, certify that I am the duly appointed Secretary of the above named Corporation and that the forgoing Resolution is a true and accurate copy of a Resolution duly adopted at a meeting of the Shareholders thereof, convened and held in accordance with the Bylaws of said Corporation and that the Resolution is now in full force and effect.

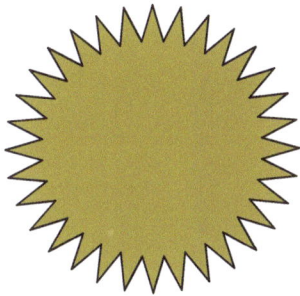

IN WITNESS THEREOF, I have affixed my name as Secretary of the above named Corporation and have attached the seal of said Corporation to this Resolution.

Dated _____ 20____

_____
Corporate Secretary

SERVICE AGREEMENT

This **SERVICE AGREEMENT** is a private agreement, entered into on this the _____ day of
_____, 20___ by and between the following Parties:

COMPANY: **(PUT IN THE NAME OF YOUR OFFSHORE IBC)**
Mailing Address: (PUT IN THE OFFSHORE MAILING ADDRESS OF YOUR IBC)
Phone: (PUT IN THE OFFSHORE PHONE # OF YOUR IBC IF YOU HAVE ONE)
fax: (PUT IN THE OFFSHORE FAX # OF YOUR IBC IF YOU HAVE ONE)
E-mail: (PUT IN THE OFFSHORE E-MAIL OF YOUR IBC.
                     IF YOU DON'T HAVE ONE GET ONE)

SERVICE PROVIDER: **(PUT IN YOUR NAME)**
Mailing Address: (PUT IN YOUR PERSONAL DOMESTIC MAILING ADDRESS)
Phone: (PUT IN YOUR PERSONAL DOMESTIC PHONE #)
fax: (PUT IN YOUR PERSONAL DOMESTIC FAX #)
E-mail: (PUT IN YOUR PERSONAL DOMESTIC E-MAIL.
                     BE SURE IT IS NOT THE SAME AS THE IBC E-MAIL)

(*Hereinafter referred to as the "Parties" or in their individual designations*).

WITNESSETH

WHEREAS, Company desires to engage the services of Service Provider to provide the
following services (*hereinafter referred to as the Project*):

"Set up" suitable domestic (United States) legal entities in the State of Nevada for Company to
undertake its lawful business and/or financial pursuits in the United States (*hereinafter referred
to as entities*).

Undertake the responsibility of "operating" said entities and "handle" all banking and other
contractual requirements that may become necessary on behalf of the entities so created and
on behalf of Company in Service Provider's personal name.

As funds are "generated" in the United States, Service Provide shall undertake investment
activity in the United States on behalf of the entities so created and on behalf of Company.

As funds are "generated" in the United States, should Company decide that no "viable"
investment opportunity exits Service Provider must wire transfer excess funds to Company for
international investment purposes until such time as suitable investment opportunities are
located in the United States.

Prepare and file all necessary applications for all required state and federal licenses and/or tax returns for each entity Service Provider "creates" on behalf of Company on a timely basis; and,

WHEREAS, Service Provider agrees to undertake the above mentioned Project for Company by whatever means Service Provider chooses; and,

NOW, THEREFORE, for valuable consideration, the sufficiency of which is acknowledged by the PARTIES hereto, on behalf of themselves and their assigns, the parties agree as follows:

ARTICLE I
SPECIFIC TERMS AND CONDITIONS

1.1. DURATION OF THE AGREEMENT: This Agreement shall be given full force and effect from the date of execution and shall be binding upon the contracting Parties for an initial period of one (1) year, commencing on the _____ day of _____, 20___. After this initial term, this Agreement shall be automatically renewed for successive one (1) year periods, unless terminated by either party as set forth herein or by the joint agreement of the Parties.

1.2. INDEPENDENT BUSINESS RELATIONSHIP: The Parties are, and shall be deemed to be independent businesses with the sole right to perform their respective services under this Agreement. Nothing in this Agreement shall be deemed or construed to create any liability for the other party whatsoever, with respect to the indebtedness or other obligations of the other Party, except as specifically set forth herein.

More specifically the Parties understand and agree that the relationship of the Parties hereto is limited to the rights and obligations as articulated in this Agreement. Furthermore, the relationship contemplated herein in no manner limits the Parties from carrying-on of their respective businesses or other activities beyond the scope of this Agreement.

1.3. LIABILITY: The parties hereto agree that with regard to the duties and/or services to be rendered by each party pursuant to the terms of this Agreement, each party shall be solely liable to anyone who may claim any right due to any acts or omissions in the performance of their respective duties and/or services or on the part of their respective agents, contractors or employees. In this same regard, the answerable Party shall hold the other Party free and harmless from any obligations, costs, claims, judgments, attorneys' fees and/or attachments arising from, or growing out of their respective services as rendered pursuant to the terms of this Agreement.

1.4. COMPENSATION: For undertaking the above-referenced Project, Company agrees to compensate Service Provider as follows:

(a)   Service Provider shall be entitled to withhold _____ (_____%) of all funds generated by the entities in the United States to "fund" a reasonable salary, bonuses, benefit plans, and all necessary company expenses. Upon Company agreeing to the amount of Service Provider's salary, bonuses and benefit plan Company agrees that should the income of the entities not permit the payment of same, Service Provider may request Company to "loan" the necessary funds to the entity(ies) in order to undertake these expenses.

_____

_____

_____

1.5.   COMPENSATION PAYMENT DATE: Company agrees to compensate Service Provider (*for the services stated in Section 4. above*) at a pre-determined time by the written or verbal agreement of the Parties:

1.6.   NON-LIABILITY TO THIRD PARTIES: The Parties individually and separately accept their individual liability for taxes, imposts, levies, duties, charges and any institutional cost(s) that may be applicable in the execution of their respective roles herein.

1.7.   INDEMNIFICATION: Each Party shall fully indemnify and hold harmless the other Party (*and its officers, managers, and/or employees*) from any and all claims, demands and liabilities, including attorney's fees and costs incurred in connection with proceedings, actions, or investigations which arise from or are related to the actions or omissions of the offending Party (including any and all representations made by the offending Party's representatives to clients regarding entity structuring, legal liabilities, tax issues, etc.).

ARTICLE II
MISCELLANEOUS TERMS AND CONDITIONS

2.1.   GOOD FAITH: Each Party shall promote and execute this Agreement with diligence, utmost good faith and loyalty to the other party.

2.2.   ATTORNEY & OTHER LEGAL FEES: Both parties hereby agree that in the event that either party commences an action at law or in equity against the other to enforce any of the terms, conditions, covenants, promises or provisions of this Agreement by reason of a breach or default hereunder, the party prevailing in any such action shall be entitled to, and receive all reasonable attorney's fees and other such costs from the other party.

2.3.   WARRANT: Each Party, and each person signing on behalf of a Party, represents and warrants that they have the full legal capacity and authority to enter into and perform the obligations of this Agreement without any further approval.

2.4.   INVALIDITY OF PARTICULAR PROVISION(S):   In the event that any portion of this Agreement shall, for any reason, be deemed to be invalid or unenforceable, the remaining portions of this Agreement shall be fully effective, valid and enforceable.

2.5.   VENUE: Both parties hereby agree that the venue for the terms, conditions and provisions of this Agreement shall be in Clark County in the State of Nevada..

2.6.   BINDING AGREEMENT: This Agreement shall be binding upon and shall inure to the benefit of the successors, assigns, personal representatives and heirs of the respective Parties hereto, and any entities resulting from any sale, reorganization, consolidation or merger of any Party hereto.

2.7.   ENTIRE AGREEMENT: This Agreement constitutes the entire understanding and agreement between the Parties and supersedes all prior agreements, representations or understandings between The Parties as it relates to the subject matter hereof. Further, all preceding agreements relating to the subject matter hereof, whether written or oral unless merged into this instrument, shall be null & void.

2.8.   NOTICES: All notices and other communications under this Agreement, must be in writing, and if mailed, must be mailed by registered or certified mail, or delivered by hand to the party to whom such notice is required to be given. If mailed, any such notice shall be considered to have been given three (3) business days after it was mailed, as evidenced by the postmark. If delivered by hand, when receive by the party, or their representative, as evidenced by a written and dated receipt of the receiving party. The mailing address for notice to either party shall be the address shown herein.

2.9.   FACSIMILE OF THIS DOCUMENT: Unless specifically referenced herein, a signed facsimile of this document shall be legally binding as though it was an original instrument. Furthermore, this Agreement shall be deemed delivered upon receipt by facsimile of a copy or copies hereof that bears the signatures of The Parties and, upon receipt by any other Party by facsimile or a copy, or copies, hereof that bears the signature of the other Parties.

2.10. ADDENDUMS & EXHIBITS: All addendums, annexes or exhibits to this Agreement shall be deemed part of this Agreement and thereby incorporated as if fully set forth herein. Failure to attach any addendum or exhibit hereunder shall not invalidate this Agreement or any addendum(s) or exhibit(s), it being understood that the same is available from the books and/or records of the other Party.

2.11. WAIVER OF BREACH: A waiver by any Party hereto of a breach of any kind or character whatsoever by the other Party, whether such be direct or implied, shall not be construed as a continuing waiver of or consent to any subsequent breach of this Agreement on the part of the affected Party.

2.12. TERMINATION OF THIS AGREEMENT: This Agreement may only be terminated by the Parties as stated in Article I Paragraph 1.1, or: (**1**) for misconduct or negligence by either Party (**2**) by mutual agreement of the Parties.

2.13. COMPLIANCE WITH LAW: The Parties to this Agreement shall each be independently responsible for performing their duties hereunder in strict compliance with all applicable federal, state, and/or local laws and/or regulations.

2.14. ADDITIONAL TERMS AND CONDITIONS:

_____

_____

_____

IN WITNESS WHEREOF, The undersigned confirm that they are the authorized representatives of their respective entities. Further, they warrant that they fully understand their legal rights and obligations in connection herewith and that having understood these legal rights and obligations, have without any reservation, agree to be bound by this Agreement as of the date first written above.

FOR AND ON BEHALF OF COMPANY:

Authorized Signatory: _____

Printed Name: _____

FOR AND ON BEHALF OF SERVICE PROVIDER:

Authorized Signatory: _____

Printed Name: _____

NOTE: DO NOT HAVE THE SAME PERSON (OR THE HUSBAND OR WIFE OF THE SAME PERSON) SIGN ON BEHALF OF BOTH THE COMPANY AND THE SERVICE PROVIDER.

Abusive Tax Schemes

Unreported funds sitting in an offshore bank account can earn interest or be used for investment purposes and can be difficult for certain taxpayers to have access to such money. These are several methods used to fraudulently get funds back to the taxpayer:

Fraudulent Loans   The taxpayer's International Business Corporation (IBC) will make a loan to the taxpayer. The funds are wire transferred back to the taxpayer's U.S. bank account. Since these wired funds are allegedly loans they are not taxable. Many times ownership of the IBC is through bearer shares so it is very difficult to prove that the loan is a complete sham.

Credit/Debit Card   One of the more popular methods in recent years has been use of the bankcard to access offshore funds. Once the foreign bank account is established, the taxpayer is issued a bank card. The taxpayer can use the bankcard to withdraw cash and to pay for everyday expenses.

These methods of attempting to hide funds offshore in a manner which is not compliant with current U.S. tax law is illegal, 'evasive' and could cause the taxpayer serious fines and penalties, or even imprisonment.

Report Suspected Tax Fraud Activity

If you have information about an individual or company you suspect is not complying with U.S. tax laws, please report the activity.

www.ingramcontent.com/pod-product-compliance
Lightning Source LLC
Chambersburg PA
CBHW041446210326
41599CB00004B/153